OPEN MY HEART TO HEAR

Hymn-Based Devotions

Compiled by Jeremy S. Bakken

NORTHWESTERN PUBLISHING HOUSE
Milwaukee, Wisconsin

Cover Photo: Lightstock
Design: Amy Malo

Northwestern Publishing House
N16W23379 Stone Ridge Dr. Waukesha, WI 53188-1108
www.nph.net

Published 2024
Printed in the United States of America
ISBN 978-0-8100-2833-3
ISBN 978-0-8100-2834-0 (e-book)

24 25 26 27 28 29 30 31 32 33 10 9 8 7 6 5 4 3 2 1

Acknowledgments

We thank the following authors for their contributions to this collection: Mark Albrecht, Jon Balge, Johann Caauwe, Charles Degner, Donn Dobberstein, Jon Kehren, Curt Lyon, Gregory Lyon, Jason Oakland, Fred Piepenbrink, Joel Prange, Paul Prange, Victor Prange, William Schaefer, Stephen Schroeder, Warren Widmann, and Jon Zabell.

These devotions were originally authored for the Hymns for Life curriculum as faculty devotions. Open My Heart to Hear *enables this rich content to reach a greatly expanded group of readers.*

Hymn references are to *Christian Worship: Hymnal* © 2021 Northwestern Publishing House.

Contents

HOLY WEEK

EASTER

HOLY TRINITY, SECOND COMING, AND MINOR FESTIVALS

TRIUNE GOD

MEANS OF GRACE

LIFE OF THE CHRISTIAN

LIFE OF THE CHURCH

INDEX

Advent

A Hymn for the Ages

"Savior of the Nations, Come" | 301

"A hymn is a child of the age in which it was written." (E. E. Ryden)

"Savior of the Nations, Come" was born out of controversy. A fourth-century Benedictine monk named Ambrose penned it, making this hymn one of the oldest in existence in the New Testament church. Ambrose spent much of his life fighting a false teaching that denied Jesus was really God. The teaching claimed that because Jesus was human, he was therefore only a creature (created by God). Therefore he did not really possess the full array of God's divine qualities.

Some of the clearest and boldest statements ever written saying, "This is what we believe!" come from times of struggle. Ambrose's legacy is an Advent hymn that expresses what we believe about Jesus and why we plead for him to come soon. We believe and sing that:

- Jesus came for all people: *"Savior of the nations"* (st. 1; Isaiah 49:6).
- Jesus was begotten of the Father: *"From the Father's throne he came and ascended to the same"* (st. 4; Ephesians 4:9,10).
- Jesus was conceived by the Holy Spirit: *"Not by human flesh and blood, by the Spirit of our God was the Word of God made flesh"* (st. 2; Luke 1:31-35).
- The incarnate Jesus was born of Mary: *"Wondrous birth! O wondrous Child of the virgin undefiled"* (st. 3; Isaiah 7:14).
- The resurrected Jesus triumphed: *". . . captive leading death and hell. High the song of triumph swell!"* (st. 4; Ephesians 4:8).

Every Advent urges us to prepare for the coming of Christ. *"Yes, I am coming soon"* (Revelation 22:20). But do not doubt or worry! Marvel and be amazed that the one who is coming is our Savior, *"the Word of God made flesh."* Reaffirm your Advent faith in the triune God. Then sing this hymn for the ages!

Prayer
"Praise to God the Father sing,
praise to God the Son, our King,
praise to God the Spirit be
ever and eternally." Amen. (st. 5)

Living Up to His Names

"O Come, O Come, Emmanuel" | 327

Have you ever stopped to consider how much pressure was on Jesus just to get it right, just to be the Messiah who had been long foretold? For years God's children had been longing for his day. They had extremely high hopes and expectations because of who the prophets said this Messiah would be. They called him Emmanuel, the "Root of Jesse," the "Dayspring from on high," the "Key of David." That's how the prophets described the coming Messiah.

And then Jesus arrived. He was hardly someone who looked like Emmanuel, God with us. Not exactly the "Root of Jesse" they were expecting. Did even Jesus himself ponder those titles when people mocked him saying, "Is this not Jesus, the son of Joseph" (John 6:42)?

I don't know if Jesus ever felt the weight of those expectations. But I do know that he never failed to meet them. If Jesus was going to be Emmanuel in every sense of the word, he had to be a true human being. If he was truly going to be the "Root of Jesse," he had to come from Jesse's line. But it wasn't just who he was that matched those titles. It was what he did. He made "safe the way that leads on high" (st. 4). He put "death's dark shadows . . . to flight" (st. 3). He accomplished all this and more by giving himself in our place and dying for the sins of the whole world.

So we sing with the ancients, "O come, O come, Emmanuel." We do so not with an uncertain hope that the returning Savior will meet our expectations but with the certainty that he already has. Our prayer is that our Emmanuel—our "Root of Jesse," our "Dayspring from on high," our "Key of David"—will come soon to bring to completion for us what he has already accomplished.

Prayer

Dear Lord Jesus, you are Emmanuel—God with us. Help us to cherish your Word, remember daily our baptism, and partake regularly of your body and blood, for there you are found. There salvation is proclaimed. There faith is formed and nurtured. There we hear you say, "Surely I am with you always. Behold, I am coming soon!" Amen.

Christmas

Songs of the Heart

"From Heaven Above to Earth I Come" | 331

Martin Luther wrote this beautiful Christmas hymn. Lutherans love to sing. They especially love to sing at Christmas. We sing because our hearts are filled with the joy of the Savior's birth. We sing to encourage one another as we worship together. We teach our children Christmas hymns so they can remember what God's Son came to earth to do—for them and for us.

This hymn invites us to join the angels who came down from heaven to announce the birth of the Savior. In a sense, we become like the angels when we tell people about Jesus. We are God's messengers. In stanzas 1-7, the angels speak to us. Stanza 2 is the highlight of that message:

"To you this night is born a child
of Mary, chosen virgin mild;
this little child of lowly birth
shall be the joy of all the earth."

Beginning with stanza 8, Luther shows us how to respond to this good news of the birth of Jesus. After the angels speak to us, we speak to Jesus. Stanza 13 is the highlight of this section:

Ah, dearest Jesus, holy Child,
prepare a bed, soft, undefiled
within my heart, made clean and new,
a quiet chamber kept for you.

Take a few moments to read through this hymn as a devotional exercise. In your devotional life, first listen to God's Word. Then speak to him in prayer. This hymn teaches us how to do that.

Prayer
Dearest Jesus, you came from heaven to earth to share our sorrows and our humanity. You came to rescue us from death and hell. All the presents in the world are not worth even one moment spent with you. Let every day be Christmas in our hearts! Amen.

Trusting Jesus for Everything

"O Jesus Christ, Your Manger Is" | 342

"Dear Christian friend, on him depend." (st. 3)

You can depend on Jesus. For what? For everything. Why? Because Jesus provides anything and everything you need. Because Jesus is with you anywhere and everywhere you are. Because Jesus can do anything and everything you need him to do. Why? Because Jesus loves with an I-gave-my-perfect-life-for-you love. The same Jesus who was born and placed by his mother in a manger in a stable is the Jesus who showed a glimpse of his almighty power by stilling a storm. No obstacle in your life is so big that Jesus can't lead you past it to safety. Every sorrow or fear this sinful world brings into your life must pass the filter of God's love. Everything he allows into your life must receive his permission to enter your life so that it works what he knows will be for your eternal good. Jesus is not your copilot; he is the pilot to take you safely toward your eternal home—through whatever you face. The same Jesus who walked this earth with the sinful people he came to save is the Jesus who is preparing a throne in heaven for those who trust him.

The little baby we come to see in Bethlehem each Christmas is God's perfect gift of love to our world that desperately needs his love. God's only Son came on God's mission of love to show a world full of unworthy sinners that God loves us unconditionally. His love is a forgiving love, a saving love. Only Jesus could make the payment that had to be made to satisfy God's justice. Because of what Jesus did, the Father has marked every sinner's record Paid in Full. "How greatly God must love you!" (st. 3).

Prayer
Lord Jesus, as I remember your humble birth, help me see your love and power at work to guide me safely though my life to the glory you have prepared for all who trust you. Amen.

Can I, Will I Forget?

"Where Shepherds Lately Knelt" | 345

"Can I, will I forget how Love was born, and burned its way into my heart—unasked, unforced, unearned, to die, to live, and not alone for me?" (st. 4)

What do you remember from school, and what have you forgotten? What do students remember the next day, and what do they forget?

One way that pastors make conversations with shut-ins is to ask them about the Christmas programs they participated in when they were children. A flood of memories comes back from those early days of church and school. The elderly who were raised in Christian families remember feeling loved by family members, by teachers, by congregation members, and by their Lord.

Even when most other things have been forgotten in old age, it is startling how many people can still recite the words of Luke chapter 2, the Christmas gospel, from their childhood Christmas programs. They do not forget how Love was born that night so long ago.

There is a temptation to view holiday preparations like the riot at Ephesus in Paul's ministry: "Some were shouting one thing, some another. Most of the people did not even know why they were there" (Acts 19:32). But do not be frustrated. The same Lord who lived and died for you, the one who entered your heart by grace alone—unasked, unforced, and unearned—is working on the hearts and minds of you and those around you by his powerful Christmas message.

A Savior has been born to you. He is Christ the Lord: a child, a Son, the Prince of peace for you (st. 3). And not for you alone (st. 4).

> **Prayer**
> Lord, lead me to find you once again with fresh eyes in the manger bed, and accept my worship and praise. Amen.

God's Gospel Characteristic

"Of the Father's Love Begotten" | 358

During catechism instruction we learn about God's characteristics. God is omnipotent, omniscient, omnipresent, and eternal. Then we can take each of those characteristics and ask, "Is this law or gospel?" For example, God is omniscient. He knows everything. Is this law or gospel? It depends on the day, right? There are days when I don't want God to know everything I've done. There are other days when I find comfort in the fact that God knows that I'm hurting. Another example is that God is omnipotent. He is all-powerful. Is this law or gospel? God has power over my fiercest enemy. I love to hear that. On the other hand, God could crush me for my sins by raising his little finger. So the characteristics of God can be both frightening and comforting.

But then we get to God's most defining characteristic: God is love. There is not an ounce of law in that truth. From the very beginning, this has always been who God is. Consider what was "begotten" of the Father's love from the very beginning of our world. "Oh, that birth forever blessed when the virgin, full of grace, by the Holy Ghost conceiving, bore the Savior of our race" (st. 2). Before time began, the Father knew that he would show us his love in this way. Before time began, God knew that he would take an undeserving young virgin named Mary and place his grace upon her by choosing her to be the mother of the Savior. Before time began, love was the driving characteristic behind everything that the Father did on our behalf.

Because of the Father's great love for us carried out through the sacrifice of his only Son, we pray:

Prayer

"Let the heights of heaven adore him,
angel hosts his praises sing,
powers, dominions bow before him
and extol our God and King.
Let no tongue on earth be silent,
every voice in concert ring
evermore and evermore." Amen. (st. 4)

Epiphany

A Star in Heaven

"How Lovely Shines the Morning Star" | 370

How would you like to have a star named after you? During a recent Christmas season, people were given the opportunity to give a name to a star up in the heavens for a fee of $50. You could send in your money and receive the paperwork to name a star after yourself or someone you designate.

There is no need for Christians to apply. We can skip all that because already our "names are written in heaven" (Luke 10:20). We know that because of the greatest Star of all—Jesus. In this hymn, Jesus is called the lovely Morning Star, and the good news is that his star becomes our star.

At certain times of the year, before sunrise in the east, you can see a bright morning star just above the horizon, announcing that the darkness is ending and a new dawn is here. The apostle Peter used that picture to describe the advent and redeeming work of Jesus. Peter reminds us that we are in spiritual darkness "until the day dawns and the morning star rises in [our] hearts" (2 Peter 1:19). Sin is what resided in our hearts from birth, and sin promised a dark day of eternal suffering and pain in hell. But when the Morning Star rises in our hearts, that is, when Jesus takes up residence in our hearts through faith, our sins are washed away in the blood that Jesus shed on the cross. He now lives and reigns in the heavens, promising a wonderful new day of eternal joy. How lovely is the Morning Star that shines in our hearts!

At our baptism, Jesus placed his name on us. There is no need to pay good money for a new star in the heavens called by our name. We can claim the name of the Morning Star. And it didn't cost us anything.

Prayer
Gracious Father, thank you for the free gift of salvation you have granted us. Keep our faith strong through your Word even unto eternal life, for Jesus' sake. Amen.

The Journey Home

"As with Gladness Men of Old" | 372

Home at last. It's enjoyable to take a trip to some nice part of the world or to visit family and friends, but after a week or two of living out of a suitcase, it is good to be home again.

Have you ever wondered what the Magi thought when they arrived home again after their trip to see Jesus? Theirs was a trip that no doubt took many months. When they left home, they didn't even know where they were going. They just followed a guiding star and trusted that it would show them the way. When they found Jesus, they knelt down and offered him "gifts most rare" (st. 3). Then they went home again.

We aren't told anything about these men after they left Bethlehem. But we can guess that they didn't just put away their stuff and forget all about where they had been or what they had seen and heard. From the way the Bible records their story, we can guess that they were changed forever. After all, they had talked to Mary and Joseph. Perhaps Mary and Joseph shared with them the visits of the angels. Joseph likely repeated to them that the child was named Jesus, "because he will save his people from their sins" (Matthew 1:21). Mary and Joseph may have told of their encounter with Simeon and

Anna in the temple, where Simeon called Jesus God's "salvation" (Luke 2:30).

So they were home again, but home would never be the same. They knew about the forgiveness of their sins. They knew that their earthly home was just a place to live for a while. They knew that God had come to earth to prepare a heavenly home for them. And now they knew exactly where they were going.

Like these Magi, we too are on a journey. We don't know all the details about the trip or what we will have to go through to get to our destination. But we know where we will end up. And so we pray:

> **Prayer**
> "Holy Jesus, every day
> keep us in the narrow way;
> and, when earthly things are past,
> bring our ransomed souls at last
> where they need no star to guide,
> where no clouds thy glory hide." Amen. (st. 4)

Game Time

"To Jordan's River Came Our Lord" | 377

It's game time. John had been preparing for this moment. It was his first start as the varsity quarterback. Before leaving the locker room, his coach put his hand on the back of John's head, pulling him close to his face. He stared straight into his eyes and said to him, "John, I believe in you. Go get it done." All the preparation in the world could not have given him more confidence than those words. "My coach believes in me . . . me!"

It was game time for Jesus. He'd been waiting 30 years for this time. But whom are we kidding? It had been more than 30 years. All of eternity had been leading up to this. Jesus called upon John the Baptist to baptize him. Why? "To stand beneath the Father's will and all his promises fulfill" (st. 2). Jesus was to be counted among sinners. But there was more. This was the beginning of game time. It was time for Jesus to publicly get to work. It was time to take a three-year journey of ministry that would lead to the cross. It was time to be publicly who he came to be—the Savior of the world. The Savior from eternity would now carry out his task.

But before Jesus hit the road, the Trinity stood together and did this amazing thing. The Godhead expresses its confidence not from some outside coach, but it expressed its confidence in itself.

As Jesus in the Jordan stood
and John baptized the Lamb of God,
the Holy Spirit, heav'nly dove,
descended on him from above.

Then from God's throne with thund'rous sound
came God's own voice with words profound:
"This is my Son," was his decree,
"the one I love, who pleases me." (sts. 3,4)

If John the Baptizer had any doubt who this Jesus was, there was only clarity now. "This man is Christ, our substitute!" (st. 6).

It's game time. With this hymn, we see Christ begin his public ministry and we give thanks because we know how this game ends. "As God's own choice, from Adam's fall," Jesus was anointed in the waters of Baptism "to save the world and free us all" (st. 5).

Prayer
Lord Jesus, when it was game time for our salvation, you did everything the Father demanded. You accomplished it by the power of the Spirit. Help us see in your baptism the truth that you are God's Son, the Savior of the world—our Savior. Amen.

Double Glory

"Down from the Mount of Glory" | 388

In Peter's second letter, he reflected on what he saw at Jesus' transfiguration. "We did not follow cleverly devised stories when we told you about the coming of our Lord Jesus Christ in power, but we were eyewitnesses of his majesty" (2 Peter 1:16). Peter witnesses that he saw the glory of God in the face of Jesus.

But there is a second glory this hymn speaks about. What is it? Jesus spoke these words at the beginning of Holy Week. "The hour has come for the Son of Man to be glorified. Now my soul is troubled, and what shall I say? 'Father, save me from this hour'? No, it was for this very reason I came to this hour. Father, glorify your name!" (John 12:23,27,28).

Just for a moment, picture the face of Jesus on the cross. He is bloodied and bruised. His face is swollen almost beyond human recognition. Do you see the glory of God in that face? Yes! You see a God who would rather die for you than live in heaven without you. You see a God who would rather take your sins into his own body than let you spend one moment suffering in hell. This "hour" that Jesus spent on the cross was the defining moment for the human race—and for you and me individually.

"Then hail the double glory of Jesus Christ, our Lord,
and let the wondrous story full peace and joy afford!
The holy mount acclaims him the majesty divine;
Mount Calvary proclaims him Redeemer—yours and mine." (st. 5)

Prayer
Lord Jesus, let me see your glory on the cross, that one day I may see your face in glory in heaven! Amen.

Lent

Grace Just for Me

"What Grace Is This" | 395

Grace has been aptly described as God's Redemption at Christ's Expense. This hymn helps us appreciate the high cost that Jesus our Lord and God paid for our redemption. God's grace in Christ costs us nothing, but it cost Jesus everything.

"What grace is this!" we sing in amazement. My Lord and King sets his face to suffering. In Luke 9:51 we are told that Jesus "resolutely set out for Jerusalem." In Isaiah 50:7 the Messiah says, "Therefore have I set my face like flint, and I know I will not be put to shame."

"What grace is this!" We stand in awe as the very God stoops to carry a cross and walk a very real road of rock and blood, a sinner's road just for me.

Though Lord of all, he yields to Pontius Pilate and offers his hands to a Roman hammer. His blood flows just for me. How rude that our God, sinless and pure, hangs on a cross with common thieves. He bleeds and sheds his blood for our misdeeds, a complete payment for all.

"What grace is this!" He allows himself to be wrapped in cloths and gently laid in a manger. He allows himself to die, to be taken down from a cross and wrapped again in cloths and laid in a tomb, just for me.

"What grace is this!" The eternal God wears his raw humility in real time and in a real place to lift me up to eternity. Such grace! Just for me!

Prayer
Blessed Lord God and Savior, we thank you for the Holy Spirit who has led us to see the depth and fullness of your suffering for our sin. We thank you for this hymn that helps us see the contrast between your greatness as our Lord and God and the depth of suffering you went through for us. Amen.

An Unknown Love Made Known

"My Song Is Love Unknown" | 397/399

How many kinds of love do you know? The love between a parent and child? The brotherly love of a friend? Romantic love that blossoms into married love? Patriotic love? A neighbor's love? Most people have experienced at least one or more of these.

There is one love that no sinful heart can know or have by human experience, and that is a love for God. We lost it when Eve and Adam started to love themselves more than they loved God. And ever since, we have been loving things and people more than we have loved God. The truth is that our sinful hearts are hostile to God and even to his love for us. His love is love unknown, and no one can know it or receive it without the help of his Holy Spirit.

But this unknown love has been made known to us in the life of Jesus. This hymn reviews for us some of the ways that Jesus made God's love known. Though Jesus was despised and rejected by those he came to save, he healed the sick, the lame, and the blind. And the greatest love of all: He went through suffering and death so that the sinful world might be set free from sin and death. The world has never known a love like this.

But what a blessing it is that this love has been made known to us! It has been documented for us in God's own words in the Holy Bible. And even though it is written down for all to read, he calls us to proclaim it. Even though people have heard it before, he calls us to a ministry that repeats it again and again. Even we who profess it need to be fed and refreshed with it.

Let us make known what the Lord has made known to us, and let us keep on making it known until everyone knows it!

> **Prayer**
> Lord, thank you for showing me how to live in your love. Fill me with your Spirit as I make your love known to others. Amen.

Remembering the Cross

"Sweet the Moments, Rich in Blessing" | 400

Take a glance at a cross hanging on the wall in your church, school, or home. If you have more than one, just pick one and take the time to think about what that cross signifies. Of course, it is a reminder that Jesus died on the cross to take our sins away. Let the cross hanging there in your house spur your imagination to take you to the real cross. That is where you can understand how our just and holy God can tell you that your sins are forgiven. He doesn't ignore them. His just holiness won't allow that. When you look at the cross, you are looking at the very location where God took the world's sin and put them all on Jesus. He did that so that Jesus could die paying for them. Sin always costs a life. Old Testament animal sacrifices pictured what Jesus would do. The cross hanging on your wall reminds you that Jesus did what had to be done. God took your sins, put them on Jesus, and marked the debt Paid in Full, even for people who don't know it yet and even for those who don't want it.

Luther said, "Where there is forgiveness of sins, there is also life and salvation." That's what makes the moments you spend contemplating the cross of Jesus sweet moments, rich in blessing. If your cross is empty, it is a reminder that Good Friday was good because sin was paid for and death and hell lost the war of the worlds. You can even look at that cross and see all the way to the heaven Jesus is preparing for you right now. "Lord, in loving contemplation fix our hearts and eyes on you till we taste your full salvation and your unveiled glory view" (st. 5).

> **Prayer**
> Lord, the cross in our home is more than a decoration. It is a reminder of all you have done for me. Don't let me pass that cross unheeding. Keep me focused and close to you. Amen.

Backwards

"Glory Be to Jesus" | 402

It seems so odd to talk about Christ's glory while we sing a Lenten hymn about his crucifixion, but that is exactly what we do. God flips everything upside down. The One through whom all things were created, who rules all things from the right hand of the Father, who can call on legions of angels with a single word shows his greatest glory when he is at his weakest. To us, it seems backwards.

But consider how it is the same with your life. The evil you encounter becomes good. The suffering you experience drives you to Jesus' cross, where you see his glory. God in human frailty becomes sin for you. The God who turns the ugly scene at the cross into "glory" promises to do the same for the ugliness in your life.

When Abel was killed by his brother Cain, his blood cried out for justice: "This is not right!" But if Abel's blood demanded vengeance, Christ's blood delivers pardon. Instead of vengeance, sin is forgiven. Life is granted. Heaven is promised. This different blood is "the precious stream which from endless torment did the world redeem" (st. 3).

So where should you look for glory? In your success? In your wealth? In your own triumphs? Perhaps we should start with the glory of Christ found when he dies in our place. This is where we find our comfort and our desire to move forward. His glory is when he becomes weak for us. Our glory is grounded in this backwards scene. So when we triumph, God be praised; and when we suffer, God be praised as well. All things are made right, even our sufferings. So "swell the mighty flood; louder still and louder praise the precious blood!" (st. 6).

Prayer

Dear Jesus, we praise you for your precious blood. Help us see your glory in the most hidden of places: at your cross and in our own crosses. Amen.

Permanent Images

"On My Heart Imprint Your Image" | 405

A tattoo—an image printed on the body—often tells what is most important to its bearer.

If you *had* to pick one image for your tattoo, what would you choose? Could you make a better choice than Jesus on the cross? That image sums up what blessed Jesus means to a Christian. "Jesus, crucified for me, is my life, my hope's foundation, and my glory and salvation."

Tattoos may be very meaningful. Or perhaps a tattoo is the result of a foolish choice made because of a drunken binge, lost bet, dare, or desire to impress or intimidate someone.

"On my heart imprint your image, blessed Jesus, King of grace" is the earnest cry of a believer asking Jesus to grow his or her faith and love for God and others. Only the gospel causes someone to see Jesus by the eyes of faith and resemble him more in character and love.

Satan will try to stop you from growing in faith. He uses life's riches, cares, and pleasures to try to do that. "Love money and things more than Jesus." "A good God wouldn't let you suffer so." "Indulge your mind and senses with life's pleasures (even through God warns you to put him above those)."

But when Satan tries to put people, things, or a life of less pain or more money and pleasure between you and Jesus, remember the image of Christ's cross and how much God loved you there.

A silversmith told someone watching him work that he had to hold a piece of silver in the hottest part of the fire and keep watching it constantly. Left a moment too long in the flames, the silver would be destroyed! Asked how he knows the silver is fully refined, the silversmith smiled. "Easy . . . when I see my image in it."

Prayer
Jesus, on my heart imprint your image. By your grace, through your Word, keep my eyes on your cross and what you did for me there. Keep my eyes on you, not on riches or pleasures. When I suffer, remind me you're always watching, matching my suffering to exactly what will shape me in your holy image. Amen.

Love and Sorrow Meet

"When I Survey the Wondrous Cross" | 407

How much does God love us? Even our children know the right answer. If you want to know the full extent of God's love, look at the cross of Jesus.

Isaac Watt's famous Lenten hymn paints a picture of what happened at the cross. There we see a mixture of love and sorrow unlike any the world has ever seen. Here is God in human flesh, willingly suffering for the sins of his creatures. What a contrast to us and to the world around us. Next to the humility of Jesus, our own sinful pride looks pathetic. Next to Jesus on his cross, all the treasures of this world look like trash. Next to the amazing, divine love of our Savior, all the other things that charm us from day to day look so empty. That's what we see at the cross.

How much does God love you? The cross of Jesus is worth far more than a passing glance.

"See, from his head, his hands, his feet,
sorrow and love flow mingled down.
Did e'er such love and sorrow meet
or thorns compose so rich a crown?" (st. 3)

Prayer
Lord God, cleanse us from the guilt of our sin, fill our hearts with the peace that can be found only in Jesus, and move us to give all that we are and have in service to him. Amen.

Holy Week

Humble Majesty

"Ride On, Ride On in Majesty" | 411

Jesus rode a donkey into Jerusalem on Palm Sunday. He came to that capital city in lowly pomp—regal majesty veiled in humility. Was this journey joyful, or was it sad? Maybe it was both. People praised him with with "Hosanna": "Save us, rescue us. You can do it. And you will, won't you?" It is a journey of joy because that is exactly what Jesus came to do. In a few days Jesus would tell those people that "it is finished." The next Sunday his empty tomb would prove it to the world.

The people of Jerusalem knew what Jesus came to do, but they didn't know how he was going to do it. Sadly, their plea to rescue them meant that Jesus had to "ride on, ride on in majesty! In lowly pomp ride on to die" (st. 2). God's Savior-Servant did just that. God's plan designated Jesus as his chosen, victorious Suffering Servant. An evil and hateful plot against Jesus accomplished what God had planned before he created the world. We are sinners. We prove it every day. God allows no sin. Jesus never sinned. The penalty for any and every sin is death. Jesus died. Jesus sacrificed his perfect life to give us the perfection God demands and to suffer the death we deserve. Jesus did all that because we could never do it ourselves. It is finished. He is risen.

Jesus' ride into Jerusalem in lowly pomp was sad because our sin was the reason that he made that trip. Jesus' ride into Jerusalem was joyful because that is what our Lord Jesus willingly did to save sinners. "Ride on, ride on in majesty! In lowly pomp ride on to die"—and because he did, we will praise him forever.

Prayer
Dear Lord Jesus, with the people of Jerusalem we praise you. You are our Savior who has rescued us from sin. Help us always rejoice that you were willing to ride on to your death so that we can rejoice with you in life eternal. Amen.

Praise in All Circumstances

"All Glory, Laud, and Honor" | 412

It has been said that some of the same people who sang "Hosanna!" on Palm Sunday demanded "Crucify him!" on Good Friday. This may or may not be true, but we can relate to the fickleness of the human race. We love Jesus when things are going well but are less than enamored when we bear a cross. With the hindsight of two thousand years, Palm Sunday is a day of mixed emotions for Christians. What a glorious scene! Yet we know what is coming. Good Friday looms.

Sweet hosannas ring from children's lips still today on Palm Sunday, sometimes as they wave palm branches. What a heartwarming thing it is to teach this hymn to children and hear them praise their King with such innocence and hope. They know he is in charge and all will be well. But we teach them also that all is well on Good Friday too. According to God's promise, we teach them also that all is well when darkness looms in their lives. And the same is true for your lives too! Jesus is the source of every blessing. He will give you what you need. He is David's Son, true heir to the throne. All creation honors him, and rightfully so. All glory, laud, and honor are properly offered to the Redeemer.

But this praise is not just for Palm Sunday. It's not just for when things are going smoothly. Be careful not to demand his crucifixion when dark clouds roll over your heads. He is still King on Good Friday. He is still King during your saddest days. He is not just an earthly king but the Redeemer who buys us back from the clutches of Satan. We were captured by the devil, ensnared in sin, and destined for death. But with his payment we are set free. This is why he is the best of all kings. This is why we trust him. This is why we in chorus reply, "All glory, laud, and honor to you, Redeemer, King"!

> **Prayer**
> Eternal King, drive away the sinful fickleness of our hearts. Replace it with faith that honors you as King of kings. Return to our hearts again and again with the peace of forgiveness. Amen.

Hosanna!—Save Us, Please!

"Hosanna, Loud Hosanna" | 413

Hosanna is a word that comes from the Hebrew language and means "Save us, please!" It rang out in the streets of Jerusalem as Jesus rode into the city. Palm branches waved and coats fell to the ground. Crowds gathered and shouted, "Hosanna!" They were looking for someone to save them, and they believed that Jesus was the one to do that. Children captured the mood of the day and joined in that prayer. They knew of Jesus' special care for them, and they happily shouted their praises.

As the people shouted "Hosanna," they were proclaiming the truth that Jesus is the Savior God promised to send. It was a prayer that was directed toward God and also toward Jesus as the Messiah. Even if the people did not totally understand the full meaning of what they were shouting, the meaning was not lost on the chief priests and teachers of the law. As Jesus entered the temple courts, he healed the blind and the lame, and the children kept shouting, "Hosanna!" And so we read, "When the chief priests and the teachers of the law saw the wonderful things he did and the children shouting in the temple courts, 'Hosanna to the Son of David,' they were indignant. 'Do you hear what these children are saying?' they asked him. 'Yes,' replied Jesus, 'have you never read, "From the lips of children and infants you, Lord, have called forth your praise"?'" (Matthew 21:15,16).

As we sing "Hosanna" on Palm Sunday, we are making the same confession and praying the same prayer as the people of Jerusalem. We know exactly who Jesus is: God's Messiah who came to deliver us from sin, Satan, death, and hell. Our prayer is "Have mercy on me, Jesus! I know my sins, and they are great. I am lost apart from you. Save me, please!"

How does Jesus answer? He marches straight to the cross. That's where your salvation was accomplished. And then Easter's empty tomb makes it certain.

> **Prayer**
> Heavenly Father, we confess with the psalmist, "I know my transgressions, and my sin is always before me" (Psalm 51:3). Hosanna, Father, according to your will. Hosanna, Jesus, by your holy, precious blood. Hosanna, Holy Spirit, by the power of your Word. Hosanna, God our Savior, for you alone are able. Hosanna, according to your promise and for the sake of Jesus. Amen.

The Triumph of the Cross

"Sing, My Tongue, the Glorious Battle" | 419

On the last Sunday before Lent (Transfiguration Sunday), many churches sing "Alleluia, Song of Triumph" at the end of the service. While the song is sung, a banner with the word *Alleluia* on it is carried out of the sanctuary. This custom is called the Farewell to Alleluia. After the high of the Transfiguration account, congregation members are hit with the realization that the next time they enter their church, the colors will be darker—purple or black. The organ will play more somber hymns. It will be Ash Wednesday, the beginning of Lent. Just as Jesus resolutely set out for Jerusalem after his transfiguration moment, so we Christians head to the same city during Lent. We put away our alleluias, our song of triumph, and maybe even our altar flowers until they burst back onto the scene on Easter morning.

The word *triumph* also occurs in the hymn "Sing, My Tongue, the Glorious Battle," which is often sung on Good Friday. Stanza 4 begins, "Faithful cross, true sign of *triumph* be for all the noblest tree." Lent begins and ends with the word triumph but in contrasting ways. It is easy to understand *alleluia* at the resurrection. That's when Christ defeated death, and his victory is our victory. But how can we sing that the cross is a triumph? We say it because this is where Christ defeated the devil, death, sin, and hell. We belonged to the devil because of our sin. Hell was our just destination, but Christ put himself in our place. So the true triumph is in the cross. We can even think about the resurrection as one chapter in the even bigger story of the cross, the final chapter. Even in our own times of suffering, we can ponder this beautiful stanza:

> Faithful cross, true sign of triumph, be for all the noblest tree;
> none in foliage, none in blossom, none in fruit your equal be,
> symbol of the world's redemption, for your burden
> makes us free. (st. 4)

Does your life seem like a barren tree without fruit, flower, or foliage? Remember the cross. That barren tree is the most beautiful tree of all. It tells us that everything is going to be fine! Why? Because that's where the glorious battle has been won. Let's sing the ending of the fray and break free of being stuck in the middle.

> **Prayer**
> Dear holy Victim, you triumphed over sin and death for us. Remind us again and again of your victory so that we may live with the peace of forgiveness and the hope of our eternal home. Amen.

A Great Burden Removed

"O Sacred Head, Now Wounded" | 428/429

Think of a sin that you still remember. Perhaps it was an angry tone of voice that made it hard for anyone to hear the love of Jesus in your words. Or a sin you promised yourself you would never do again. Or one you thought no one would know about.

When we remember sins like these, we feel a heaviness inside. It's the burden of our guilt. We cannot lift it away. We cannot make it disappear. We cannot undo the wrong we have done.

That heavy feeling of guilt can result from just one sin. But when there are countless sins, this increases the burden—a burden that rightly would have crushed us in suffering and separation from God.

That is what the burden of our sin did to Jesus. He willingly picked up this burden and carried it away from us. The prophet Isaiah describes it this way, "The LORD has laid on him the iniquity of us all" (Isaiah 53:6). This burden pressed and weighed on Jesus on Good Friday—a burden we see reflected on his sacred head, wounded by soldiers' fists and pointy thorns. Though we cannot fully comprehend the weight our Savior felt as he hung by the nails, we know why he was in that dreadful place. In our place he suffered, and for us he died. It was our burden he carried. In humble amazement we confess with the hymn writer, "My burden in your passion, Lord, you have borne for me" (st. 2). And when Jesus carried this burden, he removed it forever.

We rejoice to hear our Savior say, "The burden of your sin is no longer yours. I made it my own, and now it is gone from you. Be at peace in my forgiveness."

Prayer

Dear Jesus, we praise you with grateful hearts: "What language shall I borrow to thank you, dearest Friend, for this, your dying sorrow, your pity without end? O make me yours forever, and keep me strong and true; Lord, let me never, never outlive my love for you." Amen. (st. 5)

The Nature of Sin

"Stricken, Smitten, and Afflicted" | 430

This hymn reflects beautifully on one of the greatest sections of the Bible: Isaiah 52:13–53:12. When you read the book of Isaiah, this section stands out in every way. As you read it, you immediately ask yourself the question, "Who is Isaiah talking about?" That was the question the eunuch of Ethiopia asked Philip when Philip joined him in his chariot. It gave Philip the opportunity to tell the eunuch who Jesus was and what Jesus did for him.

The hymn challenges us with these words. "If you think of sin but lightly nor suppose the evil great, here you see its nature rightly, here its guilt may estimate" (st. 3). Isaiah 52:14 tells us that Jesus' appearance was disfigured beyond human likeness. I saw a woman once in the hospital who was in a head-on collision. When I saw her face, I thought to myself, "She doesn't look human." Jesus was beaten to a pulp, beyond human recognition.

And more. He was stricken by God himself, smitten and afflicted. He bore the punishment for our sins and endured "the stroke that justice gave" (st. 2). We cringe when we think of what Jesus endured for us, and we will never again be able to "think of sin but lightly" (st. 3).

And we will never again be able to think, "My sins are not forgiven." There is no sin that Jesus did not pay for. Isaiah said it this way: "After he has suffered, he will see the light of life and be satisfied; by his knowledge my righteous servant will justify many, and he will bear their iniquities" (Isaiah 53:11). Jesus is the sacrifice that cancels our guilt so that our hope is built on him (st. 4).

Prayer
Lord Jesus, bring me to your cross with a penitent heart that sees the real nature of my sin through the lens of your suffering and death. And then lift me up in my spirit with the confidence that all my sins have been forgiven. Amen.

All Is Finished Now

"O Perfect Life of Love" | 431

"O perfect life of love! All, all is finished now." (st. 1)

Our perfect, holy Savior spoke three powerful words from his cross. He spoke victoriously in the face of death—"It is finished." Now and forever his work is finished. Now and forever sin, death, and hell are all an unholy gang of losers. Jesus' words are just as true for us every day as they were when he first spoke them. You stand before the throne of God. Your conscience weighs you down. You regret so many things you said and so many people you hurt. Some of the guilt is thoughtless. Some of the guilt sadly comes from things you meant to say and do. What do you want to say to the holy God with the justifiable right and reason to let you live with your guilt until you die without him forever? "I'm sorry. Forgive me."

Your Lord Jesus looks at you, and you know nothing is hidden from him. He knows it all. "And on his thorn-crowned head and on his sinless soul our sins in all their guilt were laid that he might make us whole" (st. 4). "No work is left undone of all the Father willed" (st. 2). He lifts your bowed head and wipes your tears flowing from your shame and guilt. "It is finished," he says. He takes you back to

Calvary and shows you the cross again. It's empty now, and so is the tomb because "it is finished."

You know, sadly, that there will be more days when you will need to go with Jesus to that cross with still another plea for forgiveness. "Your works, O Lamb of God, I'll plead, your merits, not my own" (st. 6). Once again you hear Jesus say, "It is finished." "O perfect life of love!" (st. 1).

> **Prayer**
> Lord Jesus, you have called me so often back from my wandering. You still love me even though I go wandering so often. Until all that wandering is over, let me hear you say, "It is finished." Amen.

There, There

"God Was There on Calvary" | 433

We excitedly retell an incident we thought was hilarious. But no one laughs. Then either we or the listeners recover by saying, "Guess you had to be there." Some stories lose their oomph, their zing, their punch if you were not there when they happened.

Kurt Eggert's hymn doesn't allow for the possibility of saying "Guess you had to be there" when retelling the events of Good Friday. It is impossible to say truthfully to anyone—not to a single person anywhere, not to God himself—"Guess you had to be there" in respect to Golgotha, the "place of the skull" outside first-century Jerusalem's walls.

So we go there, confessing our complicity in putting Jesus there. We go there, lamenting the way God's justice landed not on us, as we deserved, but instead on his holy Son. We go there, recognizing both the horrible price required and the wonderful result of the sacrifice. There is no other place like there.

Did you ever wonder why the words "there, there" have been used as words of comfort, especially for a parent comforting a child? Language experts are not sure why the repetition of that word has become popular. Some think it is just a soothing sound for a child to hear. But "there, there" becomes specifically and wonderfully comforting if we are pointing to the cross of Jesus as we say it or sing it. There is God, there is the world's sin, there is love, there is life eternal. Neither Jesus nor we had to be there. But in his great love, the Father put all of us there.

Prayer

Almighty Father, in your grace you sent your Son Jesus to make his way to Calvary, where he willingly took my sin on himself and paid the price you demanded for it. The sight of what my sin did to Jesus is ugly and shameful. But it is also glorious, because by it you have restored forever the relationship between us that my sin had broken. Help me by your Spirit to always look to the cross and there see your forgiveness and love for me in Jesus my Savior. I ask this in his name. Amen.

Easter

Free From the Fear of Death

"Christ Jesus Lay in Death's Strong Bands" | 439/440

When did you understand the reality of death? For me it came in stages. Grandma put flowers on her son's grave at her country church cemetery. A teenage neighbor, who'd played with my brothers and attended our church, was killed in a car wreck. As a teen I dreamed my mom died, and I woke up crying. One after another, grandparents, church members, Dad, Mom, and an older brother died.

As a pastor I saw members die. I comforted troubled third-grade twins, who'd lost their dog and grandma and feared Mom and Dad would die next. A boy refused to enter his bedroom because the Holy Ghost would get him there. I learned the root of a woman's chronic drunkenness. She'd had a child by the man who murdered her husband. Consumed with guilt and shame, she feared to face her judge at death.

Hebrews 2:14,15 speaks painful truth. The scary tyrant, who "holds the power of death—that is, the devil," terrorizes sinners "who all their lives were held in slavery by their fear of death."

But Satan doesn't have the final word. Jesus does. Jesus' death and resurrection accomplished amazing results for all. "Since the children have flesh and blood, he too shared in their humanity so that by his death he might break the power of him who holds the power of death—that is, the devil—and free those who all their lives were held in slavery by their fear of death" (Hebrews 2:14,15).

Luther's hymn proclaims the great news Jesus' victory gives to believers. Death is swallowed up in victory. In rising from death, Judah's Lion ended Satan's power to enslave you with the fear of death. One day you will die. So what? You know by faith that the Passover Lamb's blood is painted over your door, so death's terrors will pass you by.

Prayer
Passover Lamb, you conquered death, hell, and Satan by your death and resurrection. Teach me not to fear my death, because you have set me free from its terrors. When I die, take me to be with you to the place where I will never fear again. Amen.

My Soul's Complaint

"I Know That My Redeemer Lives" | 441

About 30 times. That's how often we sing the two simple and powerful words "he lives" in this hymn. And what a host of gracious activities the resurrected Christ lives for! The hymn says Jesus lives to save us, to bless us, to feed us, to help us, to guide us, to comfort us, and to calm us. We even sing that he lives "to hear [our] soul's complaint" (st. 4).

My soul's *complaint*? What do we have to complain about? What portion of our Lord's interaction with us is grounds for complaint? Is it the part where he sent his Son to die for us? Is it the part where he guarantees full and free forgiveness of every sin? Maybe it's the place where he promises life forever in paradise with him?

No, there is really nothing for God's people to complain about. Yet God's people—including some of the people who wrote his Word—did and do complain. That's because all of God's saints are also sinners—sinners living in a sin-cursed, bondage-to-decay world. And the psalm-writing sinner-saints are the ones who voiced the loudest and most frequent complaints. Consider Asaph: "Will the Lord reject forever? Will he never show his favor again? Has his unfailing love vanished forever? Has his promise failed for all time? Has God forgotten to be merciful?" (Psalm 77:7-9).

Asaph has a whole list of complaints. But he takes them to the right place. His complaints are not off to the side grumblings about what has gone wrong. His complaints are addressed to God's face as he seeks elusive comfort. But as he muses and complains and questions, God leads him to the solution: "I will remember your miracles of long ago. I will consider all your works and meditate on all your mighty deeds" (Psalm 77:11,12).

One of the "mighty deeds" that Asaph eventually ponders is God's parting of the Red Sea's waters. The Israelites were hemmed in on all sides, with a drowning sea ahead of them and a murderous army behind them. But the Lord brought deliverance. No wonder we often recall and celebrate the miracle of the parting of the Red Sea at Easter time. Just as all looked lost and hopeless at the Red Sea, so all looked lost and hopeless at Calvary.

But "he lives"! Jesus' resurrection changes lost and hopeless to found and triumphant. Sing it 30 times. Sing it 30 million times. It is the answer to every single one of my soul's complaints.

Prayer

Dear Jesus, you live not only to hear my soul's complaint but also to do so much more! Oh, the sweet joy this sentence gives: "I know that my Redeemer"—you, dear Jesus—"lives!" Amen.

Salvation Certain

"Awake, My Heart, with Gladness" | 443

Are you going to heaven when this life is over? Do you feel *sure* of that? Do you ever feel uncertain or afraid?

It's not surprising that at times we may be a bit worried. After all, our consciences keep reminding us that we have sinned. God's law convicts us time and again—and that's a good thing. We still have a sinful nature: a stubborn, prideful nature that wants nothing to do with God and thinks it's fine on its own. That nature needs reminding that we cannot get into heaven by what we have done or not done. We are helpless and hopeless on our own! But we also don't want to dwell in uncertainty or fall into complete despair. Despair of ourselves as a means to salvation? Absolutely. Despair beyond all hope? Certainly not!

This hymn is a wonderful expression of our joyful Christian confidence in our eternal future. It rests on Jesus' death and resurrection. It rests on his promise of full and free forgiveness. It is confidence for you and for those around you with whom you share the truth of Jesus' death and resurrection for them.

What was the problem on Good Friday? The problem was that Jesus was dead. Can you imagine how the old evil foe shouted in triumph when Jesus died? For years Jesus' enemies tried to kill him. And finally they succeeded! All the hosts of hell joined in the celebration. Jesus was dead and buried!

But their triumph was short-lived. Their boast "turned to gloom" when Jesus left the grave (st. 2). He showed that he is more powerful than death itself. He is more powerful than Satan who wants to drag us to hell with him. He is more powerful than the guilt of our sin. Heaven has been opened to sinners—sinners like you and me. What Jesus did, he did for us, to bring us to be with him in heaven. That's what the word *Savior* means. He saves us from the death and hell that we deserve.

Getting to heaven doesn't depend on you, even the slightest bit. It depends on Jesus. "He brings me to the portal that leads to bliss untold" (st. 5). And that makes each of us sing, "Now I will cling forever to Christ, my Savior dear" (st. 4). Look to Jesus time and again. Your heart too will awake with gladness at Easter and always.

Prayer

Lord, I earnestly pray, "I do believe; help me overcome my unbelief!" (Mark 9:24). May your Word of promise always comfort me, always protect me, and always drive away my doubts and fears. And in your good time, bring me through death to everlasting life with you, again according to your Word of promise. Until then, may the confidence I have in you be my strength and my joy as I gladly share this hope with all I meet. Awake my heart with gladness by your good Spirit through your precious Word. In Jesus' name I pray. Amen.

A Come-From-Behind Win

"He's Risen, He's Risen" | 445

For a moment, think about your favorite sport. Some of the games you've seen were more exciting than others. The most exciting games are probably the ones where your team came back from a huge deficit and pulled ahead when the game was almost over, ultimately winning the game. Baseball, football, hockey—they all have exciting come-from-behind victories from time to time.

There is one such victory that stands out from the rest, and it has nothing to do with sports. Think about the come-from-behind victory that took place between Good Friday and Easter Sunday. When you look at those events from the enemy's point of view—from Satan's view in hell—Good Friday really did look like a good day. But Easter Sunday was anything but a celebration in hell. Now look at those days from our Christian point of view. Satan was doing battle with God. Everything happened exactly the way God planned it, not only from Friday to Sunday but also throughout the centuries leading up to Good Friday and Easter Sunday—and those plans all focused on Jesus.

The fears, the sadness, and the sorrow all change to good news when God tells the story the way he does in his Word. Jesus came, the God-man, to do God's work. And he did it; he finished it all. Jesus won! "He's risen, he's risen, Christ Jesus, the Lord" (st. 1). When you know that, those fears, sadness, and sorrow are all drowned out by the glorious chorus of God's people who know that sin and death have lost. Jesus won. He's risen! When you face those enemies, everything they try to say and do are drowned out as you and all God's people praise Jesus for the victory he has already won—the victory that is already ours. We are living a victorious life right now because of Jesus. Now life means looking forward to the victory banquet in heaven forever.

Prayer
We praise you, Lord Jesus, because you turned our tears and our fears, our sin and our shame into confident joy because of the free forgiveness you won. Help us live that victory now and rejoice eternally at the victory celebration you have prepared for all your people. Amen.

Jesus' Gracious Appearances

"O Sons and Daughters of the King" | 456/457

This hymn recalls the account of Jesus' resurrection appearances to people who were overcome by fear, sorrow, and doubt. Joyful alleluias interrupt the verses as they proclaim the changes that come when shattered lives encounter the good news of the resurrection.

First on the scene are the three Marys, having gone early that morning "to seek the tomb where Jesus lay." The angel "bade their sorrows flee" with the good news, "Your Lord will go to Galilee" (sts. 2,3).

Next on the scene are the apostles huddling together in fear behind locked doors. Jesus comes to them with his comforting words, "Peace be with you" (st. 4).

Now we see Thomas hearing the report that Jesus has risen but doubting that it was true. Jesus comes to him personally and overcomes his doubt. "My hands, my feet, my body see; and doubt not, but believe in me." The hymn captures his excited cry with the words, "You are my Lord and God" (sts. 6,7).

The scene shifts from the past to the present. Christians of every age struggle with sorrow, fear, and even periods of doubt. Jesus comes to us and removes our doubts and fears. Joyfully we sing, "Blessed are they that have not seen and yet whose faith has constant been; in life eternal they shall reign" (st. 8).

A quick search reveals that this hymn has found its way into the hymnals of many Christian denominations. We raise our alleluias with Christians of every age as we sing, "Today the grave has lost its sting!" (st. 1).

Prayer

Alleluia! Lord Jesus, we thank you for coming to us and showing us the nail prints in your hands and bringing us a peace this world cannot give. Alleluia! Amen.

Holy Trinity, Second Coming, and Minor Festivals

Wholly, Wholly, Wholly

"Holy, Holy, Holy! Lord God Almighty" | 483

When were you most aware of your sinfulness? Was it when your cheeks burned with shame as a small child caught in the act? Was it as a student when you were the very deserving recipient of a disciplinary measure? Was it when your hands were cuffed behind your back during an arrest? Was it when you saw the pain in the faces of people you hurt with your words or actions? Or will it be when you realize the bed you are lying on is soon going to be your deathbed?

We know when Isaiah was most aware of his sinfulness. It was when the mighty seer saw the vision of the Lord in the temple (Isaiah 6:1-8). Reginald Heber references that vision when he writes of cherubim and seraphim calling out "Holy, holy, holy!" around the throne of the King. The combination of those shouts shaking the building and the holy seraphim hiding their faces and feet in humility before the almighty King brought Isaiah to the moment when he was most aware of his sinfulness. If holy creatures hide their faces, what is an unholy creature to do?

Isaiah cried out in pained awareness, "Woe to me! . . . I am ruined! For I am a man of unclean lips, and I live among a people of unclean lips" (Isaiah 6:5). But then a transformation! A live coal is placed on his lips and he is told, "Your guilt is taken away and your sin atoned for" (Isaiah 6:7). He went from being *wholly* aware of his sinfulness to *wholly* aware of the holiness gifted to him by the grace of God and *wholly* eager to be sent to do the Lord's work.

May we too be wholly aware of our sin, wholly aware of his grace, and wholly ready to carry out his will.

Prayer

Heavenly Father, your holy law makes us wholly aware of our sinfulness. Your holy gospel declares us holy and our relationship with you whole again in Jesus our Savior. Your Holy Spirit moves us to acts of love and thankfulness for your whole plan of salvation. May we be wholly yours until the day we sing to you with the angels of heaven, "Holy, holy, holy! Lord God Almighty!" In the name of Jesus we pray. Amen.

The Song of Eternal Joy

"Wake, Awake, for Night Is Flying" | 486

Most people pass through periods of gloom. Worry, doubts, and loss may bring on this feeling. Gloom was certainly present among the citizens of the small German town of Unna in 1597. A serious plague had ravaged the community and about 1,300 people died. The Lutheran pastor in Unna during that time, Philipp Nicolai, officiated funerals frequently. His life might easily have been gripped by gloom.

But that was not the case. Nicolai wrote a pastoral pamphlet that he titled "Joy's Mirror of Eternal Life," to which he attached two great hymns: "Wake, Awake" and "How Lovely Shines the Morning Star." Both of these hymns resonate with joy.

Notice the expressions of joy sounded in "Wake, Awake." There is rejoicing because of the "thrilling cry" of the watchman (st. 1). Stanza 2 reports that Zion's "heart with joy is springing; she wakes, she rises from her gloom." Zion answers the joyful call of the watchman by entering the wedding hall.

The third stanza is a joyful description of that heavenly wedding feast and those "dwelling with the choir immortal." The English translation of the closing words of this stanza fails to capture what the German expresses. Literally, Nicolai wrote, "No ear has heard more such joy; therefore are we happy, *i-o*, *i-o*, eternally in joyful song."

This hymn is a cure for gloom. It transports us out of our earthly lives where we are confronted by sin and death to the joyful gathering of saints and angels at the eternal wedding supper of the Lamb (Revelation 19:9). At that celebration, gloom is nowhere to be found!

> **Prayer**
> Lord Jesus, drive gloom and despair from my life by giving me a vision of the joy that awaits me at the heavenly banquet. Amen.

Shining Light

"Rejoice, Rejoice, Believers" | 493

"Rejoice, rejoice, believers, and let your lights appear." (st. 1)

Flashlights work better in the dark. In fact, lights almost always need the dark to work. Focus your attention on the bridegroom in Matthew 25:1-16. He is coming to claim his bride. It is dark, near midnight, and no one knows exactly when he will arrive. Just make sure you have your light working.

Of course, this is a picture of Jesus coming back to this world that is dark with the selfishness and ignorance of sin. Some people will be ready for Jesus to come; some will not. It all depends on whether their lights are working. If your light is working, then you have a reason to rejoice, because the night with all the evidence and consequence of sin will all be over when the Bridegroom, Jesus, comes. When people let their lights go out, they are in just as much darkness as everyone else in the whole sinful world. Instead of having reason for joy, they have regret because falling asleep at a time as important as the arrival of the Bridegroom leaves them outside with no way in.

"Rejoice, rejoice, believers, and let your lights appear" (st. 1). That is the way to be ready for Jesus when he comes again. That is the way to let people in this dark world know that there is hope and there is a reason for joy even in a sin-sick world. The darkness won't last forever; the light will last eternally. Jesus has already won the battle over sin, death, and everything that makes this world dark. He has already fought all the darkness that sin causes and replaced it with the light of hope that we have as rejoicing, light-shining believers. Jesus is coming soon. Rejoice, believers. Shine your lights for the world to see.

Prayer

Lord Jesus, in this sin-darkened world help me always be ready for your return. Until that time, let me show the people around me the joy that comes from trusting you and everything you have done for me. Amen.

Filled With the Holy Spirit

"O Light of Gentile Nations" | 497

Are you not filled with awe at how the Holy Spirit came into the life of Simeon and led him to see Jesus as the Light of the world? Luke tells us, "[Simeon] was waiting for the consolation of Israel, and the Holy Spirit was on him" (Luke 2:25). The Holy Spirit had revealed to him that he would not die until he had seen the Lord's Christ. The Holy Spirit even moved him to go the temple on the very day that Joseph and Mary brought Jesus to the temple to be presented before the Lord. It was the Holy Spirit who moved Simeon to joyfully proclaim, "My eyes have seen your salvation, which you have prepared in the sight of all nations: a light for revelation to the Gentiles, and the glory of your people Israel" (Luke 2:30-32).

When we gather for worship with God's people, it is the Holy Spirit who leads us to see Jesus as the Light of the world. With this hymn we joyfully proclaim, "Drawn by your Spirit's leading, we come with joy and love . . . as Simeon once had waited his God and Lord to find" (st. 1). In the arms of faith we embrace Jesus as Simeon once did. With mouth and lips we receive his body and blood in the blessed sacrament.

There will be days "when life's troubles touch us" and times when "through our tears we often can scarcely sense [God's] grace" (st. 3). With the help of the Holy Spirit, we see Jesus as Simeon once did: "Our sun in darkest terror, the glory round our cross" (st. 3). And when our last hour comes, the Holy Spirit will be there as our Comforter to help us pray, "Lord, now let your servant depart in peace."

Prayer

O blessed Holy Spirit, you led Simeon to see the son of Mary and Joseph as his long-awaited Savior. We thank you for leading us to see Jesus for who he truly is and to embrace him with arms of faith. Amen.

Triune God

The Father's Care

"Children of the Heavenly Father" | 502

This is a hymn that especially touches the hearts of those with children (or godchildren, nieces, nephews, or other children with whom a close bond is shared). We would not be so attracted to it if we thought that our children were never in danger. But we know that they are. And this awareness makes us love this hymn because it reminds us who (and whose) our children really are.

Perhaps we're not always aware of the evil and dangers that swirl around us. Who knows how many dangers God has simply prevented us from ever seeing? How many catastrophes have his holy angels averted from our lives without our even knowing it?

On the other hand, at the slightest sign of danger, we worry about what might be. When a child's persistent fever doesn't respond to treatment, we struggle to remain calm and reasonable. When the slightest strange symptom appears in our body, we wonder what the doctor will say. When increasingly independent teenagers don't call home like they promised, we fear the worst. Usually, the worst never happens. But we know that it can.

Whether the situation is not as bad as we feared or even far more serious than we thought, the Scriptures are replete with the comforting news of our heavenly Father's care. This hymn weaves those thoughts together and allows us to sing the truth into our hearts. Whether we know it or not (when things are going fine), whether we would believe it or not (when things aren't fine), we need to remember that "though he giveth or he taketh, God his children ne'er forsaketh" (st. 4). After all, they (and we too) are "children of the heavenly Father."

Prayer
Dear heavenly Father, comfort us at all times with your promise that you have made us your children through faith in Jesus. And because of that fact, comfort us further with your promises to protect us and to work all things for our good. In Jesus' name we pray. Amen.

The Significance of Being in Christ

"In Christ Alone" | 510

The words "in Christ" are used together nearly one hundred times in the New Testament. As we read passages where those words are used, we can understand them as "in connection with Christ." Perhaps another way of understanding what the inspired writers are saying is to picture our relationship with Jesus like being safe in a bubble, with Jesus surrounding us completely on every side. Everything that comes into our lives has to have Jesus' permission to get to us. Think of all the wisdom Jesus uses to make sure that whatever enters our lives is exactly what he knows is for our eternal good. Everything must submit to him. Will this thing or event, bad or good, serve a purpose that harmonizes with his unconditional love for us? If it doesn't, Jesus won't let it in. If he does let it in, we can be sure it is happening because Jesus loves us unconditionally. Will this thing or event be too powerful for Jesus to manage in our lives? Seriously? Jesus died, but death itself wasn't strong enough to keep him from rising from death, from rising from the grave to rule the world in the almighty power of God. That power is ours because we are safe in Christ. Will anything, any event, sneak past our all-knowing Savior?

We know that's not going to happen. How can anything get past our Lord Jesus who is not only all-knowing but also almighty and always present everywhere?

If we think of being in Christ like being in that all-encompassing bubble with that perfect love and perfect power—the love and power of God all at work for each of us—then "till he returns or calls me home, here in the power of Christ I'll stand" (st. 4).

Prayer
Lord Jesus, when you are with us, we know that nothing can harm us or do anything against us while you keep us safe in your hands. Dear Lord, help us remember that you are always with us. Amen.

The Battle

"Crown Him with Many Crowns" | 511

"Crown him the Lord of life, who triumphed o'er the grave
and rose victorious in the strife for those he came to save.
His glories now we sing who died and rose on high,
who died eternal life to bring and lives that death may die." (st. 3)

"To the victor belong the spoils." You've probably heard that before. Those who win the battle get the prize. Whether those spoils are land or riches or resources, the winners get to keep them.

Now, what if the battle were about you and me? Not an earthly battle or campaign, but something much more important than that. What if it were a battle for our eternal life? What if it were up to us to earn our way into heaven? How well would we fare? How would that campaign end?

It would take no time at all to see the problem we would face in this battle if left on our own. Those daily sins that plague us, the pet sins that trip us up, even the hidden sins that no one else sees hiding in our thoughts—all show us what an unwinnable position we are in. We are completely unable to unlock the doors to paradise by ourselves. And Satan is right there, every step of the way, to accuse us and show us that we are unworthy of heaven.

How horrible it would be to stop at this point in the battle, thinking that we have to win our way into God's heavenly kingdom by means of our own efforts. But thank God it does not stop there! Thank God he did not leave us in that miserable, unwinnable situation. Through his love, he sent his Son to fight on our behalf. Jesus did everything that we could not do for ourselves, obeying the will of his Father for us and suffering death and hell on our behalf. What Christ earned for us by his sacrifice, he then gave to us—that is, the status of being God's beloved children and heirs of paradise. Through him we gain heaven!

May we ever praise our victor for both the sacrifice he made and for the life he has won for us.

> **Prayer**
> Lord Jesus, every day I am attacked by the devil, the world, and my own sinful nature. When the battle grows fierce—when temptation and doubt and fear and despair wield their ugly and deadly weapons—fix my eyes on you, dear Jesus. Fill my

> ears with your victorious shout, "It is finished!" Fill my heart with your peace. Soothe my soul with your forgiveness. Instruct my mind with your eternal truth. Hold me in your unfailing love. Send your Holy Spirit to fill my heart with trust in your unfailing promises. And hold before me the sure and certain hope I have through your victory over all my enemies, especially death. Grant this according to your mercy and for the praise of your name, Jesus. Amen.

Beautiful

"Beautiful Savior" | 522

Perhaps *beautiful* isn't the first adjective you would use to describe Jesus. You might consider your dear husband or wife to be beautiful, and certainly your children are! But Jesus? After all, Isaiah says, "He had no beauty or majesty to attract us to him, nothing in his appearance that we should desire him" (Isaiah 53:2). And the picture is even more ghastly when the prophet adds that "his appearance was so disfigured beyond that of any human being and his form marred beyond human likeness" (Isaiah 52:14). It would have been hard even to look at such a man! It was so horrible that people would "hide their faces" from him (Isaiah 53:3). So how can we sing that Jesus is our "beautiful Savior"?

You already know the first part of the answer. Isaiah is describing what Jesus was going to look like on the cross. That's where "he was pierced for our transgressions, he was crushed for our iniquities" (Isaiah 53:5). It was an ugly scene, terrible to look at. But that's where

Jesus became our beautiful Savior. Through his sufferings and death, he became our Redeemer from sin, death, and the devil.

But there's also another answer. Something we don't always think about is that Jesus is also the beautiful Savior of creation. In Romans, the apostle Paul reminds us that creation has also been affected by the fall into sin. "The whole creation has been groaning as in the pains of childbirth" (Romans 8:22). We no longer live in a perfect Garden of Eden. But this damaged creation will be "liberated from its bondage to decay" (Romans 8:21) when God's total work of redemption becomes visible. So Jesus is also the beautiful Savior and Redeemer of creation.

We can celebrate the fact that there is much that is still beautiful in God's creation. The meadows and woodlands are beautifully "robed in flow'rs of blooming spring" (st. 2). The sunshine, moonlight, and sparkling stars bring beauty and joy into our lives. All this beauty reminds us of our beautiful Savior and what he has done for us. But as beautiful as this world is, Jesus is more beautiful than the most spectacular panorama or gorgeous setting of the sun. His beautiful blood has cleansed us. His beautiful resurrection has preceded ours. That leads us to give him glory and honor, praise and adoration, now and forever.

Prayer

"Beautiful Savior, Lord of the nations,
Son of God and Son of Man!
Glory and honor, praise, adoration
now and forevermore be thine!" Amen. (st. 4)

Sheep With a Perfect Shepherd

"Jesus, Shepherd of the Sheep" | 551

Sheep are very helpless animals. They tend to their daily lives giving little thought to what would harm them. They like to wander, not realizing that they are headed for danger. When they are attacked by predators, they are too weak to defend themselves. They need a shepherd to keep them safe.

We are so much like sheep. We go about our lives and let our guard down when it comes to the spiritual dangers we face. We often wander from the safe green pastures of God's Word and expose ourselves to the predators of Satan and sin. When Satan attacks us with his temptations and accusations, we are too weak by ourselves to stand up to him.

Thankfully, we have a Shepherd to watch over and protect us. He is Jesus. He is no ordinary shepherd. He is the Good Shepherd who gave his life for the sheep. "By [his] blood our souls were bought, by [his] life salvation wrought" (st. 3). His perfect life and his death on the cross purchased our salvation. He came and rescued us and gathered us into his Father's flock. As a faithful Shepherd, he keeps watch over us 24 hours a day, 7 days a week. "Safe we wake and safe we sleep, guarded still by you" (st. 1). He protects us from all that would truly harm us—the physical dangers of this world and the spiritual enemies that would harm our soul. He guards and protects us so well that we can stand firm upon his promise that "none can take us from [his] hand" (st. 2).

Shepherds also lead their flocks with their voice. As our Good Shepherd, Jesus speaks to us through his Word, the Scriptures. Through the voice of his Word, he teaches us to walk after him and follow him. He calls us back to himself when we stray. He graciously forgives us and renews us. He comforts us and encourages us with his promises.

In our noisy world, there are many voices calling us to follow them. Above all, we listen to the voice of Jesus, the Shepherd of the sheep, and follow him with joyful hearts looking forward to the day when he calls us to heaven. There and then . . .

"We, in robes of glory dressed,
join th' assembly of the blest,
gathered to eternal rest
in the fold with you." (st. 5)

> **Prayer**
> Lord Jesus, thank you for your Word that guards us, leads us, teaches us to trust you, forgives us, and promises us life eternal with you. By that same Word, continue to keep us firm in the true faith, held gently yet tightly in your loving hands, until we reach your heavenly fold. Amen.

Law and Gospel

"Salvation unto Us Has Come" | 558

When all is said and done, there are only two kinds of people in the world. Our Lord identifies them in the parable of the sheep and the goats. A person is either a believer or an unbeliever, and on the Last Day there will be a separation between the two groups. When the trumpet sounds and the Lord returns, it will be too late to come to know and believe the truth that saves. Where one spends eternity is set for eternity at death, or for those still living, when judgment day arrives.

How is an eternal heavenly existence decided? The apostle Paul in his letter to the Romans eliminates one popular possibility. He writes, "No one will be declared righteous in God's sight by the works of the law; rather, through the law we become conscious of our sin" (Romans 3:20). Unfortunately, since the fall into sin, many people have put their hope in their good works as the way to heaven. In our sinful nature, we all think of ourselves as good or, at least, good enough to deserve God's eternal blessing. But Paul preaches the exact opposite! What a tragic day it will be for anyone who trusts in self for salvation! Jesus will say to them, "Depart from me into everlasting punishment." Why? Because no human being can keep God's commandments well enough—that is, perfectly—to earn a place in heaven. Everyone falls short of the perfection that God expects. The hymn says it this way: "It [is] a false, misleading dream that God his law [has] given that sinners [can] themselves redeem and by their works gain heaven" (st. 3).

But God reveals another way, a better way, indeed the *only* way to spend eternity in heaven. It is the way made possible by his Son and through his Son, our Lord Jesus Christ. The hymn continues, "Christ came and has God's anger stilled. . . . He has for us the law obeyed and thus the Father's vengeance stayed" (st. 5). Jesus lived the perfect life that we have not, and through faith in him, his innocence is credited to those who believe. He made the payment for our sins when he died on the cross and was raised to life again.

Our sinful nature ever inclines us to look at ourselves and perceive some measure of goodness. But according to God's law, we always find much sin, indeed only sin, in self. Instead, God invites us to look to Jesus, who fulfilled the law's demands and freely credits us with his righteousness. As we ponder this extraordinary truth, this amazing gift of love, may the Spirit move us ever more to serve and please him with our lives.

Prayer
Heavenly Father, in your love you have given us both law and gospel. Through the law, you reveal our great need for salvation, to which by nature we are completely blind. But in the gospel, you reveal your grace and mercy in redeeming us from what we deserve by sending your dear Son, Jesus, as the atoning sacrifice for our sin. Grant that we always trust in him, and through his merit, live in joy and peace both now and forever in eternity. In Jesus' name we pray. Amen.

Not What But Who

"My Hope Is Built on Nothing Less" | 563/564

When you think about hope, do you sometimes think too much about *what* you are hoping for?

"I had hoped the cancer would not come back." "I had hoped more students and their families would be in church this past weekend." "I had hoped the paycheck would last until the end of the month."

There is nothing wrong with hoping for these kinds of things. Sometimes things turn out the way you hoped. Sometimes your hopes are not realized. What does this mean for your hope?

When you think of hope, it is always better to think about *the One in whom you place your hope*. Real hope is in Jesus Christ. Without him, hope is nothing more than wishful thinking. With him, hope is sure. The psalm writer realized this when he sang, "But now, Lord, what do I look for? My hope is in you" (Psalm 39:7).

Jesus makes your hope sure and certain because of who he is and because of what he has done. He has loved you from eternity. He planned and accomplished your salvation. He lived a humble, obedient life for you and credits his righteousness to you by faith. He shed his sinless, precious blood as the atoning sacrifice for the sins of the world. Your hope is built on Jesus' blood and righteousness.

Now as he rules at the Father's right hand, he is preparing a place for you to be with him eternally. Nothing can stop his plan to bless you today, tomorrow, and forever. In Jesus your hope is rock-solid.

When you think about hope, think first and most of *the One in whom you place your hope.*

> **Prayer**
> "My hope is built on nothing less
> than Jesus' blood and righteousness;
> I dare to make no other claim
> but wholly lean on Jesus' name.
> On Christ, the solid rock, I stand;
> all other ground is sinking sand."
> Amen. (st. 1)

The Love of God

"God Loved the World So That He Gave" | 570

"God loved the world so that he gave his only Son the lost to save that all who would in him believe should everlasting life receive." (st. 1)

John 3:16 deserves its good reputation as the gospel in a nutshell. Seeing the reference held up on a crudely made sign at sporting events may cause us to roll our eyes, but it should not cause us to neglect this important Word of God.

When people doubt that God loves them, this verse makes it clear that God loves the world. If you are a part of the world, God loves you. No matter how bad you have been, God loves you. No matter how bad you feel, God loves you.

In fact, God loves you so much that he sacrificed for you. God the Father has known and loved his only Son with a perfect love from eternity, but he gave up that Son to suffer and die for you, to take the punishment for your sins so that you would never have to.

Afraid of hell? Trust Jesus to deliver you from it. He's taken care of everything, and he is trustworthy. He promises that the people who trust him will never suffer hell. You don't have to understand how that is even possible. Just trust him.

People who trust Jesus will have eternal life with him in heaven. Jesus defeated death and rose from the dead, so you know he can and will deliver on that promise. It might be bad now, but it gets better. Christ Jesus saves our souls from death—this is the anchor of our faith!

> **Prayer**
> "Glory to God the Father, Son,
> and Holy Spirit, Three in One!
> To you, O blessed Trinity,
> be praise now and eternally!"
> Amen. (st. 6)

For Me

"Jesus, Your Blood and Righteousness" | 573

Imagine a caricature of a little boy, maybe three or four years old. From a vantage point behind him, you see him looking at a hill in the distance. On the hill there are three crosses. That's all there is to the picture except for two words written at the bottom: "For me." That's all there is, but what a statement!

Jesus' blood was shed on that middle cross. His life was a sacrifice that paid for all the sins of the world. Because of what Jesus did, sinners can confidently stand before the throne of God knowing that Jesus will plead their cause in God's court. Jesus says, "Their sins have been washed away because my blood was shed for them; my righteousness is theirs." No matter how much sin needs to be forgiven, the blood of Jesus paid for all of it. Jesus did all that so that his people could look forward to the mansions he is already preparing for them.

Like the little boy in the picture, you look at those crosses in the distance and all those thoughts go through your mind. You think about the millions of people who know and love the Savior and live to thank him for what he did. You think about what it would be like to be in one of those heavenly mansions and spend an eternity praising God for his love and Jesus' willingness to forgive the sins of the world. Could there be anything greater than taking the time like that little boy to just sit there looking at those crosses, especially that middle cross in the distance? One thing would be better than thinking about the amazing love of God for the sinful people of the world. One thing—"Jesus has lived and died *for me*."

> **Prayer**
> Lord Jesus, when I think about what you did to forgive the sin of the people of the world, I am even more thankful that I, a sinner too, can say that you did all this for me. Amen.

The Chief of Sinners

"Chief of Sinners Though I Be" | 578

"Here is a trustworthy saying that deserves full acceptance: Christ Jesus came into the world to save sinners—of whom I am the worst" (1 Timothy 1:15). And really, who could argue Paul's point?

- He was a persecutor of the church.
- He stood by while Stephen cried out last words of mercy for those who were killing him—and Paul not only didn't prevent Stephen's execution, but he also approved of it.
- He was an avid despiser of all things Christian, traveling from town to town seeking out every follower of Jesus he could find to imprison them.

"Chief of sinners?" I'm not sure we'd disagree with Paul's self-assessment.

But as you and I sing this hymn, Paul is not on trial. The one singing the hymn is on trial. What does it matter that one person could kill a man but I couldn't? Does that make him the chief of sinners and me an under-the-radar, unknown sinner? No.

My sin is my sin. And my sin is serious. My sin keeps me out of heaven. My sin puts me at odds with my God. My sin damns me for all eternity. My sin makes me the chief of sinners. This strong proclamation of the law is not something that causes me to point the finger at Paul, coworkers, or "those other people." This strong proclamation of the law causes me to point my finger at me.

"Chief of sinners though I . . . I . . . I be, Jesus shed his blood for me . . . for me . . . for me." This strong proclamation of the gospel causes me to point the finger not at me but at Christ my Savior.

As we reflect on our own sinfulness, it can only lead to despair. But with the apostle Paul, we find our confidence, our strength, and our forgiveness in Christ.

"Chief of sinners though I be, Christ is all in all to me; all my wants to him are known, all my sorrows are his own. Safe with him in earthly strife, I await the heav'nly life" (st. 4). God's grace abounds in this wonderful hymn. Glory in it, forgiven child of God.

Prayer
Dear Jesus, though my sins are many, you shed your blood to pay for every last one of them. You shed your blood *for me*. When my conscience rightly accuses me of being the worst of all sinners, remind me of your love. Assure me that I am redeemed and forgiven and a child of heaven. Point me ever and always to yourself, my Savior and dearest friend. Amen.

Humility and Glory

"Not unto Us" | 582

"Not to us, Lord, not to us but to your name be the glory, because of your love and faithfulness." (Psalm 115:1)

Humility does not come to us easily. We like to receive at least some credit for any good that comes our way. We like to receive at least a little glory for our accomplishments. And it doesn't end with our lives here on earth. We like to think that heaven is ours, at least in part, because of the good lives we live on earth. But God's Word does not allow for self-commendation of any kind. Paul wrote, "What do you have that you did not receive? And if you did receive it, why do you boast as though you did not?" (1 Corinthians 4:7).

We need help if we are ever to make humility a way of life, and we have that help in Christ Jesus. Paul reminds us that though Jesus shared his Father's throne in heaven, he humbled himself when he took on our lowly human flesh. Though he is the immortal God, he became obedient to death, even death on a cross. Paul's admonition, then, is this: "Have the same mindset as Christ Jesus" (Philippians 2:5). So if all good, all accomplishments, and even heaven itself have a source outside ourselves, then what receives all the credit and glory? The answer is the Lord's name.

We know that the Lord's name is everything that is revealed about him. But his highest revealed virtues are his love and faithfulness. His grace chose us, his grace sent his Son, and his grace robed us in righteousness. And his faithfulness tells us that his grace will never end, even through our faithless years, yes, until our traveling days are over and done and our pilgrim feet lead us home to heaven.

So when you begin to feel the least bit proud, or when you look to your own good life and begin to think that you have somehow earned a place in heaven, turn to Kurt Eggert's hymn "Not unto Us" to find the hymn writer's humility, Jesus' humility, and your own humility. And then, let your lips sing that hymn to his glory and praise.

> **Prayer**
> Dear Lord, we give all glory and praise to you that your faithful love in Christ Jesus has secured our place in our heavenly home. Give us the humility to see that all our good comes not from us but from your grace. Amen.

Praise God for the Holy Spirit

"Come, Holy Ghost, God and Lord" | 585

For years the opening service at Northwestern Preparatory School and Northwestern College began with this hymn. In any good a Christian does, the Holy Spirit is involved. As a school year—or any task—begins, we ask the Spirt, our light and guide, to teach us to know God rightly, call him dear Father in spite of our sins, keep us free from errors of doctrine and life, serve Christ as master, and remain believers. No wonder Luther, who authored this hymn, exhorts us six times in three stanzas to praise the Lord!

We don't need the Spirit only when a task begins. We needed him to bring us to faith. We were spiritual corpses, helpless as a mound of lifeless dust before the Spirit breathed physical and spiritual life into Adam. God's Spirit breathed into our hearts by the gospel, and we became spiritually alive.

The Spirit keeps pouring amazing gifts on us. Luther asks the Spirit to unite all believers throughout the world in holy faith. The world needs more of true faith and unity! Only the Spirit, through his gospel in Word and sacrament, can do this. So praise the *LORD*—Yahweh, the God of free and faithful grace—who punishes and forgives every sin at Jesus' cross.

Luther's last request: I'm weak. Give me your power to battle bravely every trial Satan sends—especially when I die. Then I'll praise you forever after I safely ascend to heaven to be with Jesus.

> **Prayer**
> Holy Spirit, without you I couldn't believe in Jesus Christ, my Lord, or come to him. But you called me by the gospel, enlightened me with your gifts, sanctified, and kept me in the true faith. For forgiving my sins, for your sure promise to give me everlasting life, I praise you, Holy Spirit. Alleluia, alleluia! Amen.

The Shy One

"Come, Holy Ghost, Creator Blest" | 586

Which person of the Trinity is the shyest? That's an odd question, isn't it? Our God certainly isn't shy. The one who made the world and everything in it has no reason to be shy. Even the heavens declare his glory, and in our gospel proclamation we shout his name to the ends of the earth.

But the Holy Ghost (or Holy Spirit) is sometimes called the shy member of the Trinity because he spends all of his time pointing our hearts to the Father who created us and the Son who redeemed us.

This hymn, one of the oldest in the hymnal, remedies that supposed shyness by emphasizing the work of the third person of the Trinity.

Alternate names for the Holy Ghost hint at his powerful work: Creator; Counselor; gift of God; fount of life; fire of love; the soul's anointing; giver of light, love, and immortality (deathlessness). He comes to us through the means of grace: the gospel in Word and sacrament. He keeps us in the one true faith.

On the days when we feel like the devil is winning, this is our hymn to sing. The third person of the Trinity drives away the devil and fills our lives with peace. Yes, he does that by teaching us to know the Father and the Son, but that's not really because of shyness. It's because of his generosity with his gifts, and we praise him for coming to us with that generosity.

> **Prayer**
> "Come, Holy Ghost, Creator blest,
> and make our hearts your place of rest;
> come with your grace and heav'nly aid,
> and fill the hearts which you have made."
> Amen. (st. 1)

Hear Us, Holy Spirit

"Holy Spirit, Light Divine" | 593

It's not too often that we address prayers to the Holy Spirit in public worship. Most of our prayers are addressed to the Father or to the Son. The reason may be that we just don't have many examples of it in the Bible. One notable exception is on Pentecost Sunday when we hear the ancient prayer "Come, Holy Spirit."

Even if we don't often address prayers to the Holy Spirit, when we do, we pray big. We believe what we confess in the Nicene Creed: that the Holy Spirit is to be worshiped and glorified "in unity with the Father and the Son." Along with the Father and the Son, the Holy Spirit plays an important role in taking away "the gloom of night" from our hearts and turning our "darkness into day" (st. 1).

We need the Holy Spirit to work on our hearts because of what "this heart of mine" is like. Our hearts are naturally dark, guilty, sad, idolatrous, and dying. "This heart of mine" has nothing good to offer to God. It needs to be cleansed. It needs to be set free from "sin's bondage" (st. 2). And so we pray,

> **Prayer**
> O Holy Spirit, through your divinely appointed means, deliver to my heart the forgiveness, joy, and peace that Jesus won for me. In fact, "create in me a pure heart, O God" (Psalm 51:10), a new, clean, cheerful, living heart of flesh to replace my heart of stone. Forgive my sins. Increase and sustain my faith. Dwell in my heart that I may give of myself, my new heart included, to you "now and for eternity" (st. 5).

Every Need Satisfied

"Now Thank We All Our God" | 597/598

What is your most basic need today? Is it food? Is it a new roof for the house? Is it a job? Is it peace and harmony in the family? Is it comfort and hope as we deal with a sick spouse or child? You can probably add to the list.

Whatever your need, who is always there to supply it? The psalmist says, "The eyes of all look to you, [Lord], and you give them their food at the proper time. You open your hand and satisfy the desires of every living thing" (Psalm 145:15,16).

Isn't that about the most beautiful word picture ever? It's true; our gracious God has better things to do than patching up our self-inflicted boo-boos. Nevertheless, he is always near to us with his open and outstretched hand from which we receive freely and without strings attached all that we need for this body and life. He is always ready and waiting for us to pray for his help. And then God does what he loves more than anything else: He richly and daily provides everything that we need, according to his will.

But it doesn't stop there. Our greatest need is always for a stronger faith and a closer relationship with our heavenly Father. And so he sent Jesus to meet our greatest need. He sacrificed his own Son on the cross of Calvary for our sins and raised him from the dead for our eternal salvation. What could possibly be better than that? Lost and miserable sinners though we are, we are rescued to be the eternal heirs of God. Thanks and glory be to God, for he does all things well!

Prayer

"Oh, may this bounteous God through all our life be near us, with ever-joyful hearts and blessed peace to cheer us and keep us in his grace and guide us when perplexed and free us from all ills in this world and the next." Amen. (st. 2)

The Word That Overcomes Death

"How Great Thou Art" | 612

"In the beginning God created the heavens and the earth."
(Genesis 1:1)

With his omnipotent Word, God made everything. He spoke and all the vastness and complexity of the universe came into being. God made it all—from the intricacies of the tiniest hidden organisms living deep beneath the ocean's surface to the trillions of massive stars sending their light from immense distances into our night sky. And with his almighty power, God graciously sustains his creation to thrive until that time when he will bring it to an end—a time he alone knows.

But God's greatness is not seen in nature alone. Since the Garden of Eden, all of humankind has been cursed with the wages of sin. Out of pure love, our great and awesome God did the unthinkable: He sacrificed his only Son as payment for our sin. Only the fathomless power of our almighty God could conquer our greatest enemy: eternal death. As Jesus bled and died on the cross, he proclaimed, "It is finished." His suffering in hell and innocent death paid our debt in full. God's righteous demand for perfection was once and for all time completely fulfilled.

Yet the inevitability of physical death still looms like a specter over every person's heart. The certainty that death will come to us all as a result of our inherited sin still troubles us, but the sting of that death has been removed forever. Just as Jesus' tomb was empty on that first Easter Sunday morning, so also will our tombs be empty one day when our mighty Savior calls us from them to be with him forever in heaven. Then when we are reunited with those who have gone before us, we will certainly proclaim in humble adoration, "My God, how great thou art!"

> **Prayer**
> Gracious Savior-God, thank you for your almighty power and grace that sustains me here and for all eternity. Amen.

Heaven's Own Language of Praise

"Praise to the Lord, the Almighty" | 624

The Linguistic Society of America estimates that there are over six thousand distinct languages in the world. The three most widely spoken are Mandarin Chinese, Spanish, and English, in that order. Most languages are consistently used by a relatively small population. Linguists predict that in a matter of a few decades, thousands of spoken languages will be dead.

But there is one language that is spoken in heaven and on earth that will never die. It is the language of praise to God. Here is where words express truths—spoken or sung—that declare the wonderful works of God like creation, salvation, and preservation. These truths regard the Lord's impact on our daily life. He is reigning, sustaining, and ordaining. He made you, has stayed you, and shades you. He defends you, attends you, and befriends you. These are the very thoughts, words, and actions that God has taught us to believe, teach, and confess as we praise him in public worship and private devotion. They express our response to the truth that the Word of God was made flesh and dwelled among us. The Holy Spirit has filled us with the life of faith in the grace and truth of Jesus. It is new every time we think about his love.

Languages spoken by nations have many differences. But the praise that is spoken on earth by all the members of the holy Christian church sounds the same to the ears of forgiven sinners from every nation, tribe, people, and language. Praise is the one thing that unites the saints in the *church militant* on earth with the saints in the *church triumphant* in heaven. Praise God!

The next time you praise him, let your "Amen" echo as it resounds in heaven: "Amen! Praise and glory and wisdom and thanks and honor and power and strength be to our God for ever and ever. Amen!" (Revelation 7:12).

Prayer
Almighty God and Father, in you alone we live, move, and have our being. Pour out your Spirit so we may believe your promises and praise you in joy and peace, now on earth and one day forever in heaven, through your Son, Jesus Christ, our Lord and Savior. Amen.

Means of Grace

The Light of God's Word

"Thy Strong Word" | 630

In the beginning there was darkness. "The earth was formless and empty, darkness was over the surface of the deep" (Genesis 1:2). It was a darkness that could not turn itself into light. In spite of the theories of evolution, there was no way darkness could disappear by itself. Chaos would remain.

There was also darkness during Old Testament times. Isaiah wrote that people were "walking in darkness" (Isaiah 9:2). They stumbled and fell again and again. Their situations seemed hopeless as their kings and prophets failed them.

Even today, there is still darkness all around us in the world. The evidence is obvious. And human solutions have and always will fail to improve human nature and lift the darkness caused by sin.

Most discouraging of all, we must admit that there is darkness in our own lives as well. Sin is part of our nature, and we are unable to get rid of it by ourselves. We must admit that we know all about works of darkness as we struggle each day with dark thoughts and get caught up in dark deeds. Just as the darkness before creation could not turn itself into light, and just as the people of the Old Testament could not escape their darkness by themselves, so we also are unable to bring light and holiness and life into our own personal darkness.

But God's "strong Word" is able to "cleave" (cut through) the darkness, just as it did when God said at creation, "Let there be light"! And God's Word has continued to do that, clearing away not only the darkness of the original chaos but also the darkness of hopelessness and sin.

God's Word brings the light of salvation to the world through the message of Jesus Christ. God's "Word" (Jesus himself) "bespeaks us righteous" (declares us righteous) and makes us "glorious" in the eyes of God. Sin is forgiven so that a new life can begin.

Where we would fail in all our tasks and in all our striving, God's "strong Word" gives us strength for today and strength to carry out the tasks we face every day.

> **Prayer**
> Dear Lord Jesus, continue to shine your light into our lives. Overcome the darkness of sin, death, and the devil with your powerful promises. Give us strength to be your light in this dark world, that more and more may know you now and for eternity. Amen.

Working With Words

"Lord, Open Now My Heart to Hear" | 632

It's a consistent theme throughout all of Scripture: God works with words. God spoke the world into existence. God communicated with the patriarchs through words. Jesus himself made his presence known primarily through words rather than a grand display of his eternal divinity (save a few glimpses of his divinity in his miracles). The gospel writer John declared this Savior to be the Word made flesh. Should it surprise us that even today God communicates with us through words? He communicates to us through the spoken Word that he has handed down to us on the pages of Holy Scripture.

To us, it seems pretty ordinary, maybe even foolish. Perhaps God would be better off coming to us through a life-changing encounter with the divine. Ah, but the wisdom of God is to come to us in humility, through means we can hear and touch and taste. If God had come to us in his divinity, who could stand it? Rather, through the humble Word and sacraments, our Savior comes to us and bids us to listen to him. So as we come to worship, as we approach our own Bible study, we do so not primarily so that God can listen to us but so that we can listen to him. For there in his Word we encounter our Savior. There in his Word he speaks salvation into our hearts through the gospel. There in his Word our Savior draws us to himself and keeps us with him.

Let us approach our Savior where he is found with this prayer:

> **Prayer**
> "Lord, open now my heart to hear,
> and through your Word to me draw near.
> Let me your Word e'er pure retain;
> let me your child and heir remain." Amen. (st. 1)

The Word

"God's Word Is Our Great Heritage" | 640

"The grass withers and the flowers fall,
but the word of the Lord endures forever." (1 Peter 1:24b,25a)

The expression "Word of God," or "Word of the Lord," or just "the Word" occurs dozens of times in Scripture. In some instances, as in John chapter 1, "the Word" refers to Jesus. But in most cases, God's Word tells us what he has revealed about himself. It is through the Word of the gospel that we become children of God, and it is that same Word that keeps us in the faith.

The writer of this hymn text, Nikolai F. S. Grundtvig, intended for this stanza to be a fifth stanza to "A Mighty Fortress Is Our God," Martin Luther's great Reformation hymn. Stanza 4 of Luther's hymn begins with "The Word they still shall let remain." Grundtvig follows up that thought with the reminder that Christians have inherited this wonderful gift and that it is our task, our great endeavor, to share the message of that Word. This Word guides us in our life and sustains us as we face the ravages of death. The final lines of the hymn are a prayer that we keep the teachings of Scripture pure and that we continue to pass the wonderful news of the gospel to future generations.

> **Prayer**
> Lord, keep us steadfast in your Word. Fill us with the zeal to daily study that precious Word and to proclaim it to the next generation. We ask this in the name of Jesus who is the Word made flesh. Amen.

How Could I Stand Before You?

"From Depths of Woe, Lord God, I Cry" | 650

Martin Luther wrote this hymn as a metrical version of Psalm 130, a psalm that cries out for God's mercy. It was one of Luther's first hymns, and it was one he took special care in crafting. It became one of his favorites.

Luther wrestled personally with this question (asked for all humanity at the end of the first stanza): Lord, how can I stand before you? He had tried to stand before God with his own deeds, but that did not work. He went so far as to join a monastery and devote every waking moment to the service of God. But in the midst of all this, he knew the answer to his question was "I can't! I cannot stand before a holy God on my own."

From the depths of his sin and despair, Luther's hymn invites us to cry out with him and the psalmist for help. It is only by the grace of God, by a love that we do not deserve, that we are able to stand before God. By grace, for Christ's sake, God blots out our sin. His promise is that he will act in mercy toward those who cling in faith to Jesus and the payment he made for their sin. And we know he will always remain true to that promise.

> **Prayer**
> Heavenly Father, I join Luther and the psalmist by pleading, "Lord, have mercy on me." I cannot stand before you because of my sins. But as I cling to Jesus, I trust you will be true to your promise. Because Jesus stands next to me, I know he will also stand with me forever in heaven. Grant this, for Jesus' sake. Amen.

Jesus Sinners Does Receive

"Jesus Sinners Does Receive" | 654

This hymn so clearly describes the depths of despair for the sinner coupled with the great comfort of Romans 5:8: "While we were still sinners, Christ died for us." Consider these examples:

Stanza 1: There was a man who was worn down by his sin. He wanted so badly to leave it behind, but it was stuck to him like a burr from the forest that he just couldn't remove. "Here is hope for all who grieve: Jesus sinners does receive."

Stanza 2: Another man knew what he deserved and couldn't believe what he received. For his life of guilt, for the grief and shame that he brought upon his family, knowing that he would pay the consequences of his actions for the rest of his life, he still held on to this: "Who with humble hearts believe: Jesus sinners does receive."

Stanza 3: A woman felt that she should have known better. She'd been a Christian her whole life, and yet when she looked at her college years, she was embarrassed. "And now what? How can I go back to the God I had forsaken? How can I show my face in that church again?" But this truth remains: "Weary souls who lost their way are by Christ, the Shepherd, taken in his arms that they may live: Jesus sinners does receive."

Stanza 4: There was a man God called to this banquet. The man heard the pastor say, "Jesus says, 'Come to me, all you who are weary and burdened.'" Yet he had nothing to bring to God's perfect banquet but his basket of sin and guilt. God expected perfection from him, and all he had to bring to God was . . . himself, the sinner that he is. However, even in his sin he prays, "Let these words my soul relieve: Jesus sinners does receive."

Stanza 5: A woman cries aloud with King David, "I know my transgressions, and my sin is always before me" (Psalm 51:3). Even so, God's grace covers it all. The weight of guilt has been lifted. The fear of punishment has been removed. She is a child of God. "Oh, how blest it is to know . . . [I] shall be as white as snow . . . for these words I do believe: Jesus sinners does receive."

Stanza 7: There was a woman who didn't have much time left. She knew that her life on earth was coming to an end. But even as Satan attacked her in this most vulnerable state with thoughts of "Did I do enough? Will Jesus really receive me?" even then she held on to the only thing that mattered: "Dying, still to him I cleave: Jesus sinners DOES RECEIVE."

> **Prayer**
> Dear Jesus, in anguish of soul I come to you at your invitation. Show me mercy; forgive my sins. When the devil accuses me, when my guilt overwhelms me, when death draws near to consume me, comfort me with the sure promise that you receive sinners—even a sinner like me. Amen.

A Meal Like No Other

"Here, O My Lord, I See You Face to Face" | 660

Humans mark important occasions with eating. It's true of every culture in every time. Weddings and funerals, state dinners and business meals, birthdays and reunions. Just about every family reunion includes these three actions: eating, drinking, and talking. It is how we were made. We break bread to enjoy fellowship and to mark significant events.

It is not surprising, then, that when the Lord comes to us, he comes in Word and meal. When the family of God gathers, we talk. We talk about our past and our future, about our biblical relatives (good and bad!), and of course about our most famous brother, Christ. And then we dine. It is a fellowship like no other. How simple yet how profound. Heaven and earth crash together for this meal of simple bread and wine.

Yet family reunions don't last forever. We go back to our regular lives. The Sunday service of talking and dining doesn't last forever either. We walk out of church and go back to our day-to-day lives. "Too soon we rise; the vessels disappear; the feast, though not the love, is past and gone" (st. 5). But there is an eternal feast. A family reunion in heaven. A wedding supper like none other:

> Feast after feast thus comes and passes by,
> yet, passing, points to that glad feast above,
> giving sweet foretaste of the festal joy,
> the Lamb's great marriage feast of bliss and love. (st. 6)

Thus the service of Word and Holy Communion is an oasis in the midst of our desert lives. These means of grace give us the forgiveness, peace, and hope we need to not only survive this world but also thrive in it. We know all too well that perfection is not yet here, but with hope we move forward, having come "face to face" with God and having "handle[d] things unseen" (st. 1) in Holy Communion. We know that there will be a day shortly when we will see the unseen and dine with our Lord. Until then we lean on him as our strength and hope, an oasis in our desert.

Prayer

Heavenly groom, you have made your church your bride and have prepared a wedding banquet for us. Keep coming to us in Word and meal, and show us your love until we are seated at this great heavenly feast. Amen.

The Importance of Nearness

"Draw Near" | 662

The world we live in continues to grow smaller as technology and travel become more advanced. We may use these things in service to God and his Word. Great distances are spanned as churches live stream services and pastors are able to video chat with catechumens who live on the other side of the world. Certainly technology can help to get the Word out to the world.

But for some things, proximity matters. Sometimes you need *nearness*. There are no technological advances that can replace or improve upon the divinely instituted sacraments. They have to be near you. You have to be close enough to be touched.

That's a good thing. Because it was in his very real, physical flesh that Christ Jesus was given on the cross; his very real, physical blood was shed on the cross. His was no virtual pain or suffering. It was real. True, Jesus could heal a dying servant from a distance by just saying the word. But for this—this living and bleeding and dying—Jesus had to draw near. He had to come into our flesh. He had to come close enough to be our substitute in every way.

And so now we draw near to him in the sacrament. At the altar we receive from the Lord his own body and blood. He is near enough for us to taste and to touch. He puts his body on our tongues and allows us to taste his shed blood. There is no confusion for whom this blood was shed and for whom this body was given. It is for us, right here.

Prayer
Dear Jesus, draw near, draw near! "In this great feast of love be with us now." Amen. (st. 4)

The Joy of Jesus

"Soul, Adorn Yourself with Gladness" | 663

The world knows what it wants: "I just want to be happy!" Bobby McFerrin's 1988 hit song, "Don't Worry, Be Happy," struck a deep chord with many.

To what sad lengths sinners go to obtain happiness! Work until you drop. Chase money and things. Sculpt, starve, stuff, train, and medicate your body. Numb your mind. Pursue every pleasure God meant for good—often to excess. Chase false gods or every new philosophy under the sun. Promising joy, Satan employs a plethora of such idols to lead souls from God into deep misery here, and ultimately, *everlasting* "unjoy" and "ungladness."

What causes earthly sadness? Simply put: sin. Mine. Yours. Loved ones'. Strangers'. The consequences of sin negatively altered every area God gave to bring humans joy: creation, life, love, spouses, kids, bodies and minds, sex, food, work, possessions, the arts, athletics—even the pursuit of God! Instead of giving lasting joy, sin fails to deliver what it promises. Instead we get guilt, shame, unmet expectations, worry, sinful anger, discontent, and death.

What an amazing gift of grace when a sinner knows "Jesus, joy of [our] desiring!" (st. 7). What he did to give us the joy of sins forgiven wasn't free for him. It cost his bitter sufferings and death. But when he gives us free forgiveness through faith, joy results, even in a sin-filled world. Got joy? Got Jesus?

What gives the joy of Jesus? The good news! So come, meet Jesus in his Word. Remember your baptism. Take Jesus' true body and blood often. The Holy Supper is a visible gospel he offers, so you will know and believe you are forgiven. Our brains can't grasp how the God-man's body and blood coexist with bread and wine. But eat and drink it, believe it, and your generous Savior will adorn your soul with gladness.

> **Prayer**
> Lord, give me true joy by telling me again I'm fully forgiven. Give me again your body and blood. Assure me you love me by allowing me to eat this holy meal at your altar. As Israel got to eat of some of the sacrifices with you in the house of worship, give me the same joy to eat this faith-strengthening meal with you, so I realize how much I am loved. Let me feast here now so I can feast with you forever. Amen.

Many Feasts

"At the Lamb's High Feast We Sing" | 675

What a privilege it is to unpack the powerful images in this hymn. It focuses our attention on Jesus the Lamb of God, who suffered for our sins and then rose victorious to give us the feast of all feasts.

Isaiah the prophet predicted the coming of this great feast with these words: "On this mountain the LORD Almighty will prepare a feast of rich food for all peoples. . . . On this mountain he will destroy the shroud that enfolds all peoples. . . . He will swallow up death forever. The Sovereign LORD will wipe away the tears from all faces" (Isaiah 25:6-8).

So in this hymn we feast on the victorious and risen Christ "who has washed us in the tide flowing from his pierced side" (st. 1).

We further feast on the victory over Satan with the words "Mighty Victim from the sky, hell's fierce pow'rs beneath you lie" (st. 5). This high feast celebrates the seed of the woman, the Lamb of God, the victim who was bruised by Satan but is now victorious in the fight. Satan is crushed beneath his feet (Genesis 3:15).

This hymn offers more feasting as we celebrate the victory that is ours over death. "Now no more can death appall, now no more the grave enthrall; you have opened paradise, and your saints in you shall rise" (st. 6).

With this feast of all feasts, the feast of Jesus' resurrection, comes the daily joy of being free from sin. So we sing, "From sin's pow'r, Lord, set us free, newborn souls in you to be" (st. 7). Someday soon we will gather together around the throne of the Lamb. We will join our brothers and sisters who have been washed in the blood of Lamb singing, "Salvation belongs to our God, who sits on the throne, and to the Lamb" (Revelation 7:10).

This festival hymn ends with a glorious doxology praising Father, Son, and Holy Spirit, who so carefully prepared for us a feast of all feasts.

Prayer

"Father, who the crown shall give,
Savior, by whose death we live,
Spirit, guide through all our days,
Three in One, your name we praise. Alleluia!"
Amen. (st. 8)

Life of the Christian

I Am Baptized Into Christ!

"God's Own Child, I Gladly Say It" | 679

Do you sometimes wish you had been born into a different family—a family with money, status, celebrity, or power? Just think of the benefits you would enjoy if your parents were royalty, billionaires, movie stars, or part of the political elite! You might think you would have it all—everything you ever dreamed of.

This hymn poses an important question: "Do I need earth's treasures many?" (st. 1). I know the answer, but I still benefit from the reminder. Earth's treasures may satisfy for a time, but eventually they will prove worthless. What I really need is someone who can pay the debt I owe for all the times I valued earth's treasures above God and his will. That someone is Jesus. "He, because I could not pay [my sin debt], gave my full redemption price" (st. 1). Jesus paid with his life the debt I owe. And it is in the waters of Baptism that Jesus came to me and united me to himself. He freely brought me all the blessings of salvation, blessings that will never fade or go away, but will last "to eternity" (st. 1).

So what a joy to say and sing, "I am baptized into Christ!":

- When my sinful failures to keep God's law disturb my soul, I find comfort in the good news that "I am baptized into Christ." (I am forgiven!)
- When Satan accuses me with my guilt, when he tries to get me to doubt God's love, I can say to him, "I am baptized into Christ." (Satan, you cannot separate me from God's love!)
- When the thought of death steals away my joy, I can recall my baptism and declare to myself, "I am baptized into Christ." (I will leave the sadness of this life and inherit the joys of paradise!)

Remember your baptism, because in those waters your gracious God connected you to your Savior, Jesus. He made you his redeemed and forgiven child, an heir of eternal life! Remember who you are in Christ—forgiven, free, and heaven-bound! With this assurance, you can look sin, Satan, and death in the face and gladly declare that you are "baptized into Christ." You are "a child of paradise" (st. 5).

Prayer
Heavenly Father, what a gift of love my baptism is! May your Word of promise, given with water, always fill my soul with joy. When conscience accuses, Satan attacks, and death draws near, remind me of the absolute certainty that I am your child, and fill my heart with peace. Grant this for Jesus' sake. Amen.

Trust in a Sure Promise

"Christ Is with Me" | 681

"We were buried with him into death,
that as he was raised by God's glory,
we might walk in life made new by grace;
having died with Christ, we shall live with him." (st. 1)

Buried and raised with Christ. That's Baptism. In Baptism, the sinful nature is drowned and life is made new in Christ. Do you always notice and feel that? Actually, your life might not always feel very new, but you can take God at his word that it is.

Even in daily life, you find yourself trusting things you cannot see. For example, the money in your purse requires that you trust the government. Imagine a government that backs up its currency with a promise that it will never lose its value. You'd be happy to have money like that in the bank. But are you sure you can trust that promise?

How much better to trust something that can never fail! That's what you have in your baptism. Baptism promises that you have been washed and made completely clean in God's eyes. It promises that you have the righteousness of Jesus covering all your sin, the sin you were born with, the sins you committed in weakness, and even the sins you didn't know you committed. Baptism promises that your sins have been buried in Christ's tomb and that you have a new life before God because of Christ's resurrection.

It's true that you do not always see or feel the blessings that God promises in Baptism. But this is a promise you can depend on: "Christ is with me everywhere I go; never to leave me, this I know" (refrain).

Prayer

Heavenly Father, by your promise I am clothed in the righteousness of my Savior Jesus through the waters of Baptism. Though I may not always see it or feel it, lead me by your Holy Spirit to believe and trust your promise that I have been completely cleansed and brought to newness of life in Jesus. You are with me everywhere. You will never leave me. Grant this for Jesus' sake. Amen.

Ownership

"Take My Life and Let It Be" | 695/696

"I want to do it myself!" "Let go; that's mine!" When we were little children, we probably had not been talking very long before we started saying things like that. From early on we discovered ways to make ourselves the center of attention. No one had to teach us how to be selfish or to enjoy the fact that we had something someone else didn't have.

When we get older, we still easily follow that pattern. "It's my money." "It's my time." "It's my happiness." "It's my life." But after getting what we think will make us happy, why is it that so often we still feel empty or want even more? Could part of the answer be that those things are not really ours?

God, who created us and all that exists in the universe, says, "The earth is the LORD's, and everything in it, the world, and all who live in it" (Psalm 24:1). What's more, God, who paid the redemption price to rescue us from sin and selfishness, says, "You are not your own; you were bought at a price" (1 Corinthians 6:19,20).

God, who gives life and new life in Christ, gives us a new way to view our lives. Our time is not our own. We cannot add even a single hour to our lives. Each day is a gift from God. Health and strength and abilities are all God's gifts, freely given because he is gracious and merciful. It is by grace that we have a place as a child in God's family, and that compels us to gladly live for him who died for us and has been raised again. It's not ours. It's all his.

May God bless and strengthen us to live ever, only, all for him.

Prayer
"Take my life and let it be
consecrated, Lord, to thee;
take my moments and my days,
let them flow in ceaseless praise." Amen. (st. 1)

Walking in Jesus' Light

"I Want to Walk as a Child of the Light" | 713

Do you always know exactly where you're going? Jesus does. Do you know what is going to happen in future minutes, hours, days, months, or years? Jesus does. Facing the future can be frightening. People worry about what is going to happen. People sometimes think only about the bad things that might happen. It's like being lost on a dark road in an unfamiliar place. That can be frightening. Still, you keep heading into the future whether you want to or not.

At times like that, think about what it means to be a child of the light. The light is Jesus. Stars have guided sailors and travelers for centuries. Jesus is the star that will always lead us the right way. Jesus is the light that makes darkness disappear. We're not just following the light; we're in it. When Jesus is giving us directions for our lives, we know exactly where the star is leading us.

Every day we are one day closer to heaven where Jesus wants us to be. Every day he walks with us so that even the obstacles and the dangers, the good things and the bad things are part of our safe journey with him from now to heaven. That's a little difficult for adults to believe. Adults know something about obstacles and dangers, good things and bad things. Adults have felt pain. Adults remember what all that is like. Jesus knows all about that too. When Jesus says, "I know," he really does know. That's why we want to walk as children of the light. With the simple and unshakable trust of a child, we know that there is nothing to be afraid of. Jesus knows where he's going. And we're going along.

> **Prayer**
> Lord Jesus, every day gives me a reason to be afraid. Let me walk with you; then I know I will always be safe. Your love for me and your power to save are all I need for a safe trip through life. Amen.

Take It to the Lord in Prayer

"What a Friend We Have in Jesus" | 721

There is no shortage of self-help out there. From advice columns to radio shows to books by the hundreds, everywhere you turn there is a place to go to receive guidance in just about every aspect of our lives. People become desperate to find answers to their problems or fill voids in their lives. They yearn to find someone to listen to them and to help them when their lives are in trouble.

Unfortunately, trouble visits our lives more than we would like. Pain and sorrow, grief and loss are not only a possibility, but for most of us they are also a daily reality. The consequences of living in a sinful world leave us looking for help and answers to fix the pain and find a place to turn when our lives are turned upside down.

The hymn writer tells us precisely where to turn in the middle of all this turmoil, and that is Jesus. Not only that, he reminds us that NOT turning to Jesus at these times only ADDS to our troubles. After the hymn writer tells us that it is our *privilege* to take our burdens to Jesus in prayer, he says, "Oh, what peace we often forfeit, oh, what needless pain we bear, all because we do not carry everything to God in prayer!" (st. 1).

Forget self-help books, forget advice columns, and forget even well-meaning friends. God's Word tells us to bring our troubles to Jesus. In him we have a Savior who knows everything about us, loves us, and knows what is best for us. God himself says to us in Psalm 50:15, "Call on me in the day of trouble; I will deliver you." What wonderful peace of mind to know that God not only *allows* us to come to him with our cares and burdens, but he also *wants* us to. He says to us, "I know you. I know all your troubles and worries. More important, there is nothing that is too big for me, nothing that I cannot handle. I love you, and I will take care of you."

> **Prayer**
> Thank you, Jesus, for leading us to peace as we rest in your almighty arms. Amen.

Who Will Work?

"Hark, the Voice of Jesus Crying" | 745

Jesus said, "The harvest is plentiful, but the workers are few. Ask the Lord of the harvest, therefore, to send out workers into his harvest field" (Luke 10:2).

When Jesus wants us to pray for "workers," it may sound like he is looking for people who have special qualifications to do this harvesting. This hymn points us in a different direction. Stop and think. "Who's it gonna be?" "Who will go and work today?" (st. 1).

Have you considered that *you* are the answer to this prayer for workers? As a teacher of God's precious lambs, as a parent to children, as a friend pointing another to God's promises, as a person concerned at heart for the eternal soul of your neighbor—anytime you share God's Word of Truth with the people around you, God is moving you through his Spirit to be the answer to that prayer.

The double blessing is that as we share God's Word with others, the Spirit in turn moves them to be the answer to that prayer. Each day—in every subject we teach and all other aspects of our Christian walk—we model and practice speaking the truth in love, using God's Word to teach, rebuke, correct, and train God's people.

But if we're honest, we don't always do this willingly. In our weakness, we sometimes don't do it period! Every one of us can name a time, indeed many times, when our own interest in the moment was more important than God's Word of Truth that a soul next to us needed to hear. There are many times when the Spirit has opened the door to conversation about God's love for sinners, but we have failed to recognize the opportunity, or worse, chosen to not even pursue it. Not only is the harvest plentiful around us, but it is also plentiful inside us. Sin that needs rebuking and confessing; repentance that needs the assurance of God's forgiveness in Christ.

And so we pray as Jesus instructed, "Lord, send workers into the harvest fields!" He sends pastors and Christian friends to harvest the fields of our hearts with his law and gospel, and we in turn with them. And by the Great Commission, God sends all believers as the answer to this prayer. So many souls need to hear God's gospel truth. So many need to hear it again and again.

Prayer
Lord of the harvest, you sent your Son, Jesus, to redeem all people. It is your heart's desire that all come to know and believe the truth, that all would spend eternity with you. Send workers into these ripe spiritual fields! Help us to be among those workers—willingly, joyfully, and faithfully—until you return again. In Jesus' name we pray. Amen.

Beginning Tasks

"With the Lord Begin Your Task" | 776

This is the perfect hymn for the beginning of the school year. We hear it sung so often that we can often overlook the deeper meaning of the words. What does it mean to begin our tasks "with the Lord"?

The Lord is omnipresent—always with us—but the prayer of this hymn is that he would be with us in a special way. When we gather around his Word, even just two or three of us, he promises to be with us in that special way, and when he is with us like that, special blessings follow.

The hymn writer knows those blessings. They include salvation and the calm cheerfulness and joy that come from being confident our sins are forgiven through faith in Christ Jesus. Those blessings include protection from temptation, foes, ills, and the disasters that would befall us without the Lord's constant protection. Even when there are obstacles in the course of our lives, we look forward to the joy of living in the mansion that God is preparing for us in heaven.

It doesn't hurt to sing this hymn at the end of the day, the week, or even a school year as well. Our lives and tasks go on everywhere, and we want the Savior's blessing to follow us no matter where we go or what we do. Begin and end your tasks with the Lord, and confidently look for the good that follows.

> **Prayer**
> Lord Jesus, we know that only what you bless prospers. Be with us in our lives of service to you and to others with your protection, guidance, and blessing. Strengthen us by your Word of promise, and bring us safely through the day to a place of peace and rest. We ask this in your saving name. Amen.

Beginning the Day With God

"Father, We Praise You" | 778

Morning comes and it's the same thing every day: We think about what we will be doing today. We know some of it will be unpleasant. We go about our morning routine and glance at the news. Things aren't much different from what they were yesterday. Most of the news is bad. That is not a good way to start the day. When we start the day that way, we can't wait for the day to be over, and we know that tomorrow we'll do it all again. There must be a better way to start the day. Yes, there is a better way to start the day.

All too often we think about God and our relationship with him only when we need to think about him—when we're sick, scared, or struggling. But we need to think about our relationship with God at the beginning of every new day. When we think about our Savior, the greatest gift our loving God has ever given, when we remember the Easter miracle when our Savior rose, then we have God's love and power with us to face any new day no matter what might happen, good or bad. We can say with confidence, "My God will be with me all day." That's a whole better way to begin the day than hoping that the morning routine will be better today than yesterday or the news will be better than it was yesterday. The love and power of God is at work for us every day all day long. Think about that—first thing every day.

When we start our day with God on our mind, we're practicing trust in God that will bring us safely to our eternal home. Jesus is there now preparing our place. We want to be ready when he decides it's the right time to bring us home. The right time is all the time when we know God is always with us and we know we're always with God.

> **Prayer**
> Dear heavenly Father, remind me that you are always with me and let me stay close to you every day. Amen.

Commending All Things

"Luther's Morning and Evening Prayer" | 782

Every time I take off in an airplane, I whisper this prayer: "Into your hands I commend my body and soul and all things." The same prayer is offered up each night as I fall asleep. When the plane lands safely and when I awake for another day, I thank the Lord that he has kept me from all harm and danger. For who knows what tragedy might have come to me on that airplane or what dangers lurk outside of my home at night? Though I take steps to be as safe as possible, my safety is ultimately out of my control. It is all in the hands of a loving heavenly Father.

Even more serious than the physical dangers we face every day are the spiritual attacks of the evil one—Satan—who would like nothing better than to wrest us out of the hands of our heavenly Father. And so we pray for the holy angels to attend us as they did to Jesus when he was tempted in the wilderness (Matthew 4). Since Jesus defeated Satan once and for all on the cross of Calvary, we too can face the assaults of Satan with the confidence that the victory has been won for us.

All of this leads thankful believers to live God-pleasing lives that are reflective of the love that has been shown to us by our Savior. May God give us the strength to do that day after day!

> **Prayer**
> Dear Lord, keep me from the harm and danger that surrounds me each day. Make me strong to ward off the attacks of Satan and live a life reflective of your love. In Jesus' name I pray. Amen.

Remain

"Abide with Me" | 783

"Remain in me, as I also remain in you.
No branch can bear fruit by itself;
it must remain in the vine. Neither can you bear
fruit unless you remain in me." (John 15:4)

Jesus told his disciples, "Remain in me," and then added, "as I also remain in you." We have the promise that Jesus is already abiding and remaining in us. He said to his disciples just before he ascended into heaven, "I am with you always" (Matthew 28:20). So why would any one of us, through Henry F. Lyte's famous hymn, ask Jesus to "abide with me"?

It's true that Jesus is always with us and in us. But in our busy, hectic, and sinful lives, we don't always acknowledge his intimate presence. We don't always look for guidance in his Word. He is our Great High Priest, but we don't always seek his comfort and help in prayer. He remains in and with us, but we don't bear as much fruit as we could if we consciously and consistently remained in him.

So this hymn is a prayer that Jesus would abide with us so that we may do a better job of remaining and abiding in him. When other helpers forsake us (st. 1); when we are discouraged at how the world is falling apart (st. 2); when we are desperate for peace and forgiveness (sts. 3,4); when we need help resisting the tempter's power (st. 5); and when we face our final enemy in death (st. 6), then Jesus' abiding presence is needed to help us remain in him.

When Henry Lyte finally set this hymn to music in 1847, he lay dying from tuberculosis. He lived only three more weeks. But in his last stanza, you can picture Jesus as his closest companion when he writes: "Hold thou thy cross before my closing eyes; shine through the gloom and point me to the skies. Heav'n's morning breaks, and earth's vain shadows flee; in life, in death, O Lord, abide with me!" (st. 7).

Prayer

Dear Lord Jesus, remind us daily that you abide in us so that we might always remain in you and bear the fruit you desire. Amen.

At Day's End

"Now the Light Has Gone Away" | 784

After a busy day, many of us look to evening as a special time. The tasks of the day can be put aside. We can relax our bodies and quiet our minds. The closing of the day gives us a chance to ponder the bigger things of life. We can reflect on how our day has gone, and we can ponder the things of God. If we are outside, we can look at the stars and be amazed at the majesty and power of our God who made them all and set them in their places.

As the sun goes down, we may also think about the passing of time and the fading and fleeting nature of this world and this life. In the evening we have time to reflect on how we have lived our lives during the day just past. We remember the wrongs we have done and the good we have failed to do. We also begin to think about the day ahead, perhaps worried and anxious about the challenges and troubles we may face the next morning.

Unfortunately, our modern evenings so often interfere with such thoughts. Lights from computer monitors, TVs, and cell phones distract us after the sun goes down and steal from us the time for thoughtful reflection. But some of our evening still needs to be dedicated to our God, pondering who he is and how good he is to us, confessing our sins to him, thanking him for the blessings of the day, and entrusting ourselves to his care and keeping.

May the words of this hymn serve as a fitting prayer as you come to the end of your day.

> **Prayer**
> "Now the light has gone away; Father, listen while I pray, asking you to watch and keep and to send me quiet sleep.

"Jesus, Savior, wash away all that I've done wrong today. Make me ever more like you, good and gentle, kind and true.

"Now my evening praise I give; you once died that I might live. All your precious gifts are free—oh, how good you are to me!" Amen. (sts. 1,2,4)

Peaceful Sleep

"Now Rest beneath Night's Shadow" | 794

"Lord Jesus, since you love me,
O spread your wings above me
and shield me from alarm.
Though Satan would assail me,
your mercy will not fail me;
I rest in your protecting arm." (st. 3)

Bed should be a sanctuary, a place for quiet rest. But children think monsters are hiding under it, tweens have night terrors, and adults wake up in the middle of the night in a cold sweat.

When our consciences assail us, we might be able to fall asleep. But anxiety awakens us after a short time, and falling asleep again seems impossible. Satan comes with his accusations, and no matter how we try to distract ourselves, our minds return to what we have done wrong or what we have neglected to do.

Only the forgiveness of sins won for us by Jesus on the cross can cleanse our guilty consciences and give us peace. Jesus' perfect life in our place gives us the right to approach God's throne of grace with confidence.

"Now Rest beneath Night's Shadow" is the song of a believer. We believers do not always feel right. We do not always sleep well. But we are always able to speak in faith to our own souls (sts. 1,2), to our loved ones (st. 4), and especially to our Lord Jesus (st. 3).

> **Prayer**
> Dear Lord, send me sweet slumber. Bid your hosts attend me, and through the night, watch over my bed. Amen.

Lambs That Need a Shepherd

"I Am Jesus' Little Lamb" | 804

Sports teams sometimes choose animals, birds, and insects as their team name. Lions, eagles, hornets, lambs . . . Wait—lambs? Nobody chooses to call a fighting team lambs! Cute and cuddly, lambs would never exemplify fierceness, fighting to the finish, like so many other animals would.

God calls his Christian team lambs. How fitting! From our first moment in our mother's womb, we're anything but powerful. Helpless, defenseless, not so bright, prone to stray. Easy marks for predators to target, kill, and eat. Lambs desperately need a shepherd to lead them to good pasture and water, treat them for disease and pests, and protect them from wild beasts and rustlers. Straying lambs need a shepherd who will work relentlessly to find them when they stray.

The name of lamb fits sinners to a T. Left to ourselves, our life would be a relatively short, greased slide into hellfire. We sorely need a Good Shepherd.

And thankfully, we have one perfectly equipped for the job. Jesus knows what we need. He's got the power to provide. He knows our names and loves us. We can't roam beyond his influence. No physical or spiritual enemy or danger can outwit, overpower, or defeat him. He rescues us from every danger, even when we choose to wander into it.

He does those needed good things for his lambs by his Word and sacrament. They give us his constant love. They give us the joy we have in Christ because of his forgiveness.

This hymn ends with a picture to remember. The lamb, safely home in heaven, is resting in the loving arms of the Good Shepherd.

> **Prayer**
> Jesus, my Good Shepherd, you laid down your life for me. Keep giving me all I need. Keep me well-fed, strong, safe, and spiritually alive through the good news and protection of your Holy Word. Amen.

No Need to Worry

"Do Not Let Your Hearts Be Troubled" | 809

It happens all the time. We're worried. We don't know what to do. We look for someone who will calm us down. We talk to a good and trusted friend. The understanding advice that comes almost automatically is "Don't worry. Everything will be all right." That is probably something we've heard, maybe even said. Does it help? We know the care and concern, but there is still a problem. Can that good friend really *do* anything to make things all right? At best there are probably too many limitations that ultimately lead to "There's nothing I can do" or "I can't make it completely and perfectly all right."

Before we ever get to that point, we would do well to remember that the place we really need to go to with worry and fear is Jesus. He has told us not to worry. The difference is that he tells us why we don't need to worry and *shows* us why we don't need to worry. He has a goal for our lives, a goal that we may forget about sometimes. Jesus never forgets that bringing us safely to his heaven with him forever is the only goal that really matters. He is the way to that goal and what he tells us is the truth. That truth means our eternal life. We know how Jesus proved he loved us. He lived to give our lives meaning. He died to make our death a glorious entry into life as God planned it to be. His resurrection means our perfection before God, body and soul eternally. So he says to all his people, "Do not let your hearts be troubled." That's not a well-intentioned wish from a good friend. It is the Word of our Savior who has already won all our battles for us.

Prayer

Lord Jesus, help me remember that every time of need in my life is an opportunity to trust you because you are the Way, the Truth, and the Life. Amen.

For Me Personally

"I Am Trusting You, Lord Jesus" | 816

*"I know whom I have believed,
and am convinced that he is able to guard
what I have entrusted to him until that day."* (2 Timothy 1:12)

Catechism students learn that saving faith in God involves three essential ingredients: knowledge, assent or acceptance, and trust. Knowledge comes as a person is taught God's Word. Acceptance is announced when one makes a confession of faith. But the trust part is a lifelong struggle that requires God's daily help.

Trust personalizes your faith. Trust is not just that God has justified the world but that God has justified me. Trust is not just that Jesus is the friend of sinners but that Jesus is my friend. Trust is not just that Jesus answers prayers but that Jesus answers my prayers. Notice how the personal pronoun "I" is repeated in Frances Havergal's hymn "I Am Trusting You, Lord Jesus." She personalized her knowledge and acceptance with a rich measure of trust that all of God's promises in Christ Jesus applied directly to her. Her trust included salvation (st. 1); pardon and cleansing (sts. 2,3); guidance (st. 4); power, especially to witness (st. 5); and, in general, all that God offered her in Christ Jesus (st. 6).

David wrote, "I trust in your unfailing love; my heart rejoices in your salvation. I will sing the LORD's praise, for he has been good to me" (Psalm 13:5,6). A growing trust in the Lord results in a rejoicing heart, which naturally leads to an outburst in song. That song may very well be Frances Havergal's hymn "I Am Trusting You, Lord Jesus." We would be wise to memorize this hymn early in life and rejoice to sing it regularly.

Prayer
Lord Jesus, you have provided me with every spiritual blessing for my temporal and eternal good. Give me the grace to better enjoy those blessings with a rich measure of trust that they are all mine. Amen.

Eternal Consistency

"O God, Our Help in Ages Past" | 820

Have you ever been horribly sick but did not realize it until it was over? Your more rational side tries to convince yourself to take the day off, but you power through it anyway, since it is more of a pain to prepare someone else to cover the work for you or to make up the work later than to come in sick. In the middle of the day, you feel like you are at your wit's end and will never feel healthy again. But then the illness subsides. You recall the severity of your ailment, but you realize that, in the grand scheme of things, it was just a small segment of time.

The hymn "Our God, Our Help in Ages Past" is based on Psalm 90 and reminds us of those times of sickness. Psalm 90 reads as if Moses is reflecting late in his life on what has happened and how God had preserved him through the stormy blasts of his life. There were many moments throughout his journey that Moses seemed to be at his wit's end and unable to withstand it anymore as he led the Israelites across the desert. Yet every time he was on the other side of it, he was able to rejoice and thank God for preserving his life. Moses professed the timeless consistency of God's divine attributes—Creator, protector, and sustainer of life. Moses realized that his own time here on earth was as short as the watch that ends the night in comparison to God's timeless existence. Moses then took his reflection a step further and asked God to help him find joy in his earthly afflictions too, as they would soon be forgotten like a dream once he entered eternal life.

There are many afflictions we endure throughout our earthly lives—illness, a furious student or parent, or a strained relationship with a colleague or family member. In the moment, those difficulties feel enormous and endless. May we rely on God for shelter and protection during those stormy blasts. May we also, like Moses, rejoice in those afflictions, realizing that they are as short as the watch that ends the night compared to that ever-rolling stream of time in eternity.

> **Prayer**
> O God, our help in ages past and our hope for years to come, be our guard while troubles last until we reach our eternal home. Amen.

Treasure Hunting

"Jesus, Priceless Treasure" | 823

"The kingdom of heaven is like treasure hidden in a field. When a man found it, he hid it again, and then in his joy went and sold all he had and bought that field." (Matthew 13:44)

Few of us will ever experience the euphoria of finding an actual earthly treasure, mainly because we fail to take three necessary steps. First, we need to actively seek a treasure. Treasures usually don't just show up on our doorsteps or fall into our laps on their own. Second, we need to recognize a treasure when we see it. Some treasures have languished in attics collecting dust or are sold at auctions for mere pittance, because their owners did not realize what they truly had. Third, we need to make the sacrifices necessary to obtain the treasure, whether that means laboriously digging in a mine or venturing to the bottom of the sea.

In his hymn "Jesus, Priceless Treasure," Johann Franck describes all three steps when it comes to finding spiritual treasure. First, actively seek it: "Ah, how long in anguish shall my spirit languish, yearning, Lord, for thee?" (st. 1). Second, recognize the treasure for what it is: "Hence, all earthly treasure! Jesus is my pleasure; Jesus is my choice" (st. 4). Third, accept the sacrifices involved when gaining the treasure: "Pain or loss or shame or cross shall not from my Savior move me since he deigns to love me" (st. 4).

Have you taken the necessary steps to find your spiritual treasure? Do you actively seek him? You do when you diligently search the Scriptures and by them possess eternal life. Do you recognize Jesus as that treasure? You do when you see him as your Lord and Savior and yourself as his chosen one. Are you ready to make the sacrifices necessary to benefit from the treasure? You do when you suffer any kind of cross that comes as a result of your love and trust in him.

After seeking, recognizing, and sacrificing, by God's grace, then comes lasting euphoria, or as Johann Franck writes, "Thou art still my purest pleasure, Jesus, priceless treasure!" (st. 5).

Prayer

Lord Jesus, may we always seek you through your Word, recognize you as Lord, and sacrifice for you as our priceless treasure. Amen.

Lead Me Home

"Precious Lord, Take My Hand" | 835

It was a telegram that no one could even begin to fathom. He was on a trip from Chicago to St. Louis. His pregnant wife waited behind. Then the unfathomable telegram came. "Hurry home. Your wife just died." She passed away giving birth to their child. How does one even begin to process the emotions? Especially a man so dedicated to his Lord? The baby survived but only for two days. There is an absolutely gut-wrenching picture of the funeral . . . a mother and her child side by side in the casket.

Thomas A. Dorsey, a devoted disciple of the Lord and prolific writer of gospel hymns, was now faced with the trial that so many have faced before: questioning his Creator. Experiencing a loss of this magnitude leaves a person with questions that no one wants to face. Questions like "Does God love me?" "Does God even care?" "How could God allow such a thing to happen?" "Is God really good?" "Is God even real?"

When God's people bear crosses, it can empty us so that all that's left is to call out to our Savior and leave it all in his hands, crying for the Savior to take us home. And that is exactly what Thomas Dorsey did, penning the hymn "Precious Lord, Take My Hand" shortly after this tragic loss.

Why does this hymn hit the hearts of so many? In this world marred by sin, we know loss, heartache, burdens, guilt, and our own personal sins. With Dorsey, we know what it is to be tired, weak, and worn by the storms of life and the darkness of sin. But in this broken world, we also know a precious Lord who loves us and who takes our hand and leads us home.

Prayer
Dear Lord Jesus, the wages of sin is death, and that stark reality looms constantly and will eventually come to each of us. When death touches those we love, or finally us personally, comfort us with the sure promise that you have not only taken our hand but also purchased our soul. Grant us your Holy Spirit to trust in you, our Good Shepherd who sees us through every dark valley. Amen.

Keep Calm

"Jesus, Still Lead On" | 842

How many of us have seen at least one version of the Keep Calm posters? Keep Calm and Eat Chocolate; Keep Calm and Drink Coffee; Keep Calm and Use the Force. This now waning trend stemmed from a morale-boosting poster created in 1939 for the British government's Ministry of Information to use as propaganda during the World War II. Both historically and in present day, the Keep Calm slogan represents the bearer's perspective.

As Christians we could create our own version of the slogan to reflect our faith—Keep Calm and Follow On. In this sin-filled world, there are so many things that prevent us from keeping calm. Whether it is propaganda in the media, strained relationships with friends and coworkers, or even the words and actions of our own family members, there seem to be endless reasons to not remain calm. Yet no matter how dreary and cheerless life seems, we follow the one who reminds us that there is nothing to fear in this world. In Isaiah 43:1 we are reminded, "Now this is what the Lord says—he who created you, Jacob, he who formed you, Israel: 'Do not fear, for I have redeemed you; I have summoned you by name; you are mine.' " God gives us faith and hope that focus on the life that matters—eternal life. God never promised that life on earth would be easy for us, but he does promise to be with us through it all. "Surely I am with you always, to the very end of the age" (Matthew 28:20).

> **Prayer**
> "Jesus, still lead on till our rest is won;
> and although the way be cheerless,
> we will follow, calm and fearless.
> Guide us by your hand to our fatherland."
> Amen. (st. 1)

Every Single One!

"It Is Well with My Soul" | 850

You've packed the bags. You've loaded the car. You've made sure the kids have all their snacks and toys. You've completed all the items on your checklist and finally begin your long road trip. Several hours into your trip, however, a thought pops up in the back of your mind. *Did I forget to unplug the iron?* Or maybe it was *I think I may have left the oven on*. You now wrack your brain trying to remember definitively whether or not you had taken care of such items, all the while envisioning a smoldering fire or a burnt-down house.

What do you do? Perhaps you risk it, figuring it's only a small chance that you left those things on and an even smaller chance that it's going to result in a horrible fire. Still . . . that thought continues to tug at you. You cannot get rid of it until you know for sure one way or another that your house is not in danger. It would be hard to enjoy a vacation while worrying about what you will find when you return home. That thought would continue to weigh on your mind.

What about other areas in your life? What about those moments in your life when your sins stir up feelings of guilt and shame and you are just glad that no one else knows about them? Things you may have done and thoughts you may have had that by all rights condemn you in the presence of your holy Father?

Rest assured, these are sins—along with the sins of the entire world—that Jesus took upon himself. There was no partial payment for them, but rather a complete, perfect payment once and for all and for all time. That one payment makes us God's children again. What a beautiful message, what great comfort this is for us. Just as the hymn writer says,

"My sin—oh, the bliss of this glorious thought—
my sin, not in part, but the whole,
is nailed to the cross, and I bear it no more:
praise the Lord, praise the Lord, O my soul!" (st. 3)

Prayer
Thank you, Jesus, for giving us the assurance that ALL our sins, even the most stubborn ones, have been completely paid for by you. Amen.

Life of the Church

The Perfect Church

"The Church's One Foundation" | 855

The third stanza of this hymn references "those that hate" the church. Do you know someone who hates the church? What does this person understand the church to be? Many who hate the church are thinking of a local congregation or perhaps a church denomination. We must confess that local congregations and denominations are not perfect, and this may at times turn people off and cause them to hate the church.

What most people fail to understand is that there is a church that is perfect, a church completely pure and holy, a church built on the one foundation that is Christ. This is the holy Christian church, the communion of saints.

Sometimes we may find ourselves being quite critical of our own congregation and the people who are its members. When we start thinking that way and perhaps become upset, it's good for us to think about what this hymn says about the church. This hymn glorifies the church. That church is one; it has one Lord and one faith, partakes of one holy food, and possesses one hope.

In contrast to earthly congregations and church denominations, the holy Christian church "ever shall prevail" (st. 3). That's because its one foundation is Jesus Christ. This church is his new creation, his holy bride. He bought this church with the price of his own blood. To belong to this church is not something we deserve. Rather, it is a great honor and privilege granted to us by grace. May we daily give thanks for the blessings we enjoy because we are members of this holy Christian church.

> **Prayer**
> Lord, you are the foundation of the one church to which I belong. Help me to cherish this truth and share this truth with others. Amen.

The Triune Defender

"Lord, Keep Us Steadfast in Your Word" | 862

"Lord Jesus Christ, your pow'r make known,
for you are Lord of lords alone;
defend your Christendom that we may
sing your praise eternally." (st. 2)

The enemies of Christians are numerous and powerful. Other religions use the power of the sword to threaten the lives and livelihoods of faithful believers in Jesus. False teachers inside visible Christian churches threaten the Bible's central teaching of justification by faith. People who are trying not to feel guilty about their sins change the laws and threaten Christians who speak out against these changes. The devil, the world, and our own sinful flesh conspire to make us doubt what God has said.

When we feel the strength of our enemies, we call on God the Father to convert them. If they will not be converted, we call on God the Father to restrain them.

When we feel helpless in the face of spiritual assault, we call on God the Son to defend us by his powerful Word. When we sing his praises, we bask in the forgiveness of our sins through faith in him.

When we feel torn up by the strife and arguing around us, we call on God the Holy Spirit to bring peace and unity on earth. If others will not live in peace, we call on God the Holy Spirit to give us eternal peace.

> **Prayer**
> Lord, keep us steadfast in your Word. Amen.

One Little Word

"A Mighty Fortress Is Our God" | 863/864

So often we only believe what we can see. If we can't see the power of God on display in our lives, sometimes we begin to question whether he's really there. And doesn't that same attitude also apply to our dealings with Satan and his demons?

Hollywood has, we might say, romanticized Satan. We are drawn to this dark world of movies and stories about demon possession. That amazing, otherworldly power is scary, but strangely fascinating. But when Satan doesn't attack that way, do we tend to wonder whether he's really there? I sometimes wonder if we forget or disregard how terrifying the power of Satan really is.

Just think of it: apathy toward the sacraments, indifference to God's Word, a lack of care for the truth of the gospel—that's how Satan so often attacks you and me. Not as a fire-breathing dragon but as a subtle voice of human reason and sinful pleasure.

But now, consider the strength and power that Luther describes in his famous Reformation hymn "A Mighty Fortress Is Our God." With the dangers that we face, we need the strength that only God can provide. We need the defense that can only come from him. And he gives it to us so simply . . . "one little word," if you will.

How insulting to Satan that what it takes to defeat him is not majestic, magical, or otherworldly tools, but he is defeated with a simple word of forgiveness through faith in Jesus Christ proclaimed by mortal flesh and blood. Simple bread and wine and water are connected with God's Word, and Satan stands no chance. This gospel is so simple, but the gospel is all we need. Satan can "scowl fierce as he will, he can harm us none. He's judged; the deed is done; one little word can fell him" (st. 3).

> **Prayer**
> Dear Jesus, with your powerful Word you claim us as your own and defend us from the attacks of Satan. Help us to so know and cherish your Word that, by your grace and for your name's sake, we stand firm against the devil until we reach our eternal home with you. Amen.

Leading Us Home

"For All the Saints" | 880

Why? That is a question that seems unending to parents of two- or three-year-old children. Ten-year-olds want to know why they have to go to bed so early. Teenagers want to know why they can't use the car or go to that movie. When will it end? Why me? Why now? Why him? Why her? Why this? Asking that question usually means that we don't understand why something is happening and we don't like it either.

We know that God is leading us to eternal joy with him, but we know the road to that eternal joy is difficult. We can be sure that God loves us no matter what, that God's almighty power is working for us, but there are times when that is so difficult to see and feel and understand. It's especially important to remember God's truths and promises when standing at the grave of a loved one. We know that death was not God's idea, that it was the result of human rebellion. Still, when we think back over the life of a Christian loved one, we may get a glimpse of the ways God was at work bringing one of his saints to eternal glory. This saint fought the good fight, but Jesus won the war.

Right now, we are still fighting the good fight that Jesus has already won. As we think of a God-loved saint brought safely to God's side, we can see a picture of what God is doing for us right now. Life is a fight. Sin makes it a fight. Sin causes death. But Jesus turned our death into a joyful, victorious entrance into a full understanding of the love and power that were at work all the way through our lives leading us safely home. Amen! Alleluia!

Prayer
Lord Jesus, keep my eyes clearly focused on the victory celebration that the saints who have gone before me already enjoy. Keep me strong for the daily fight and ready to join the celebration. Amen.

Cross Now, Glory Then

"Lord, When Your Glory I Shall See" | 884

How can a good God let his dear child suffer so? Adam and Eve probably asked that too after their fall into sin brought them such bitter consequences. Learn God's answers to that question from the "Sweet Singer of Lutheranism," Paul Gerhardt.

Gerhardt, born in 1607, lived through the Thirty Years' War, doctrinal strife, and excruciating poverty, hunger, and plague. His parents died when he was a teen. His wife died too after the couple had already buried four of their five children. A loyal Lutheran, Gerhardt was removed as pastor because he refused to compromise his correct Bible beliefs. Talk about suffering!

In such trials Gerhardt dispensed God's comfort richly after he came to know by experience the theology of the cross. That is, Christians can't expect glory and pleasure here on earth; heaven is our home. Expect instead the dear cross. The motto on Gerhardt's portrait in Lübben described him well as "a theologian strained in Satan's sieve." Gerhardt's more than 125 hymns, many written powerfully and personally in the first person, eloquently and pointedly speak God's gospel comfort to hurting hearts. No wonder so many of Gerhardt's lyrics have been translated into English!

A hymn most likely to bring us to tears of joy is Gerhardt's "Lord, When Your Glory I Shall See."

This single stanza transports us to that day when we die or Jesus returns. Will we feel guilty, afraid to face our judge? No. Our sin is gone, cast off like filthy rags into a garbage can. No shame, no stench of our sin remains; Jesus' blood covers all of them. We will stand pure before our Bridegroom, dressed in *his* righteousness—like the most beautiful, radiantly gowned bride who ever walked the aisle, beaming with joy, as she walks to the altar to meet her groom.

Prayer

Dear Bridegroom, thank you for rescuing me at the cost of your suffering and death. When I'm hurting, turn my eyes to the glory waiting for me when, as your beautiful bride, I will stand in joy beside you. Amen.

Refreshing Sight

"Jerusalem the Golden" | 889/890

"There is the throne of David, and there, from care released, the shout of them that triumph, the song of them that feast." (st. 3)

The fatigue of teachers is a unique fatigue. At a certain point in the school year, the students in every classroom are tired of one another, and any teacher's patience is tested. There are certain expectations from without and within that never seem to be quite met. Inadequacies are exposed again and again no matter how much a teacher enjoys the work.

Even if you are not a teacher, you can relate to such fatigue—discord in the family or workplace, patience tested, unmet expectations and demonstrated inadequacies. At those times it is the delight of a Christian to consider a time of rest that goes beyond even vacation. Because of the life, death, and resurrection of our Savior, we look forward to an end of weariness, oppression, and care. Call it Jerusalem, Zion, or a sweet and blessed country—heaven is our home.

And what a home! Joy, glory, and bliss are there for every soul. We will be in the presence of Jesus, the Lamb of God who takes away the sin of the world. No matter how well we sang on earth, our voices will blend in beautiful harmony with the angels and all believers.

We are not in heaven yet. But the sight of it, just the sight of it, refreshes us as we do our careful work to bring others to it through Jesus Christ our Lord.

> **Prayer**
> Jesus, in mercy bring us to that dear land of rest.
> Amen.

At Your Word

"Blessed Jesus, at Your Word" | 919

"At your Word" means "at your calling" or "at your direction." With this hymn we come before our Lord and into his presence as if to say, "Lord, you called us to be here. You said we could do this." And indeed, we would never have come if he had not invited us. Why would we? Who could believe that we can come before a holy God and stand in his presence? Who would want to be this close to God? After all, "all our knowledge, sense, and sight lie in deepest darkness shrouded" (st. 2). When we come close to God and his Word, the darkness of our sinful lives is exposed. The bright light of his Word tells us that we are not worthy to be here.

But notice the first two words of the hymn: "Blessed Jesus." That immediately tells us that "we are gathered all to hear" not only condemnation for our sins, deserved though that is, but also a blessing (st. 1). "Blessed Jesus" stirs our hearts with the sweet teachings of the gospel. His Word brings the light of his forgiveness and salvation into our dark lives.

When we cry out in repentance and faith, "blessed Jesus" hears our prayers and praises, and our worship is sanctified and made pleasing to the One who has called us here.

And now we can leave our time of worship with renewed confidence to face our challenges. Things do not always go the way we would like. That is true in our life in general; it may also be true as we prepare and teach the children who are entrusted to us. A good prayer for those times is in stanza 4 of the hymn: "Grant that we your Word may trust." As we teach this Word, the Holy Spirit will make it effective according to his will.

Prayer

Blessed Jesus, when we enter your holy presence, we exclaim with the prophet Isaiah, "Woe to me! . . . I am ruined!" (Isaiah 6:5). Your law exposes every dark recess of our hearts and minds. But in your mercy you wash us clean and declare us innocent, through your blood and on account of your merit. Therefore we bless your name. Help us to share your blessed name with joy as we live as lights in your world. Grant this for your name's sake. Amen.

Abide . . . Because You Promised!

"Abide, O Dearest Jesus" | 924

The terrified toddler, unable to sleep, clutching a blankie in a death grip, pleads, "Mom, stay with me." Divorce looming, a spouse cries desperately, "Don't leave me!" Facing the imminent death of a loved one, the soon-to-be survivor demands angrily, "Don't die on me now!" In the movie *E.T.*, Elliot, realizing his alien friend would soon leave earth, interjects "Ouch." Or "I can't bear it if you leave. Stay with me!"

Juliet called the saying of good night to Romeo a "sweet sorrow" because she'd rejoice to see him again. But all too often, parting brings *only* sorrow.

Can you imagine how the Emmaus disciples felt that first Easter? Jesus lifted them from the pit of despair by explaining what the Old Testament was all about. When he was about to say good-bye, they urged him, "Abide with us."

We can promise people we'll never leave them, always be there for them, and always have their back. Sometimes we really mean it and keep those promises for a lifetime. But then death intervenes.

Only Jesus always keeps every promise. "Where two or three gather in my name, there am I with them" (Matthew 18:20). "Surely I am with you always, to the very end of the age" (Matthew 28:20). Greek can heap up multiple negatives. In Hebrews 13:5, God promises literally: "Never will I leave you. Never, never, never will I forsake you." Jesus' lambs can walk through the valley of the shadow of death without fear, because they can say to their Good Shepherd, "For you are with me" (Psalm 23:4).

It's a great blessing when one sinner assures another frightened, lonely sinner, "I'll be there for you." Better by far are the assurances of our God, who has forgiven our sins and conquered death for us, "I'll never leave you." That's why we pray and sing confidently, "Abide, O dearest Jesus."

> **Prayer**
> Jesus, I'm afraid—abide with me. I'm helpless—abide with me. I'm sinful and need your grace, Word, light, protection, and love—abide with me while I live, when I die, and forever. Amen.

God's Hug for You

"Go, My Children, with My Blessing" | 930

It is amazing what a hug can do. It releases tension, builds trust, heals loneliness, elevates our mood, and can even create happiness.

Have you gotten a hug today from someone in your life?

Now get ready for a hug from God. Long ago he told the first high priest to express his love for the people with a blessing on their heads: "The LORD bless you and keep you; the LORD make his face shine on you and be gracious to you; the LORD turn his face toward you and give you peace" (Numbers 6:23-26).

God's hug continued when the Great High Priest, Jesus Christ, came in person, embraced our humanity, and graciously demonstrated God's love that brings us peace: "While we were still sinners, Christ died for us" (Romans 5:8). After his resurrection, when Jesus visibly left this world in the presence of his disciples, "he lifted up his hands and blessed them" (Luke 24:50). This blessing still remains for us as he sends us out into all the world.

These words of blessing still come from the mouth of God, no matter who speaks them or where they are read. They work like a hug at the end of a worship service or after our first devotional time of the day. Think of it: In love's baptismal river, you are God's own child forever; through the story of his Son, he has touched you with peace and purity; through the holy meal, you are fed and nourished for a life of increased love and improved service.

Enjoy God's hug. Then hug someone who needs his love.

> **Prayer**
> Lord Jesus, may I be filled with your blessing as I bless others in your name. Amen.

Celebration

"This Is the Feast" | 938

Our culture understands the concept of a celebratory feast. Students celebrate their birthdays with treats. We go out to eat for anniversaries. When family members return home, we make their favorite foods. Families have their culinary traditions for Thanksgiving and Christmas.

But our culture does not understand the concept of celebratory worship. When outsiders observe our acts of worship, they see a few people singing unpopular songs, sometimes off-key, someone reading from an old book and making remarks that may or may not interest the listeners, and then eating and drinking small portions of bread and wine that are supposed to give nourishment to their eternal souls in the same way that beef and potatoes sustain their mortal flesh. It doesn't make any sense.

The resurrection of Jesus from the dead changes acts of worship from nonsense to celebration. As Christians gather every Sunday, they are celebrating the day that Jesus rose. The Word of God is nourishment for our souls. The Supper brings us the real presence of our risen Lord. Word and sacrament are the feast of victory!

When we feel our spiritual energy waning during the week, we look forward to the feast that we celebrate with our fellow believers. Nothing that we do to prepare for worship is wasted time. Our personal and family devotional times are all healthy snacks, hors d'oeuvres that get us ready for the main feast: the feast of victory.

> **Prayer**
> Jesus, our risen Lord and Savior, we sing with Christians across all time and space, "Blessing, honor, glory, and might be to God and the Lamb forever." Amen. (st. 4)

Have Mercy on Us, O Jesus!

"Lamb of God, Pure and Holy" | 947

John the Baptist is a memorable personality in the Bible. We recall locusts and wild honey, clothes made out of camel's hair, and him spending a lot of time living in the wilderness. We find him already in the womb leaping for joy when he heard the words of Mary. As an adult, he called out religious leaders for their hypocrisy and baptized people in the River Jordan.

But what we appreciate the most about John the Baptist is his pointing finger. When Jesus made his appearance at the Jordan River, John pointed to him and said, "Look, the Lamb of God, who takes away the sin of the world!" (John 1:29).

That key message of the Bible cannot be repeated often enough. Jesus was pure and holy. Nevertheless, he suffered on the cross. Patiently, he endured scorn and ridicule. Because he did not deserve to suffer, he was able to credit his suffering to our spiritual account. He carried our sins, paying the eternal price for them by suffering hell: separation from God the Father.

Without that work of Jesus, we would live in despair. John the Baptist's finger points us instead to the One who gives us mercy and grace, promising us that we will never suffer hell. Instead, we live in forgiveness and look forward to heaven.

> **Prayer**
> Dearest Jesus, you are the Lamb of God who takes away the sin of the world. You are MY Lamb of God who takes away MY sin. May your peace always be with me, O Jesus! Amen.

Index

Hymn Index by Title